SPIRITUAL CONNECTIONS

SPIRITUAL CONNECTIONS

Living in the Flow of God's Love

Nora Martin Spurgin

For information:
Circles of Angels Publications
circlesofangelspublications@gmail.com

Production and creative:
jonathangullery.design@gmail.com
Cover photo by Amir Esrafili on Unsplash

FIRST EDITION

ISBN Print: 979-8-9859010-0-9
ISBN Ebook: 979-8-9859010-1-6

Printed in the United States of America

To my loyal husband, Hugh,
and our wonderful children
whose love has enriched my life,
and to those who have
been lights along the way.

Contents

"Born as the eldest child into a Mennonite farm family in rural Pennsylvania, Nora evolved to become the beloved elder sister in the global spiritual community founded by Korea's Reverend and Mrs. Sun Myung Moon. This gripping memoir is a profound elaboration of the "path of light" Nora walked, and of the providential connections God made through her."

W. Farley Jones, Esq.
Former President of the Unification Church in America

"As a seamstress, craftswoman, organizational leader, counselor, missionary, author, wife, mother, grandmother, and friend, Nora is the proverbial multi-talented and effective "woman of substance." In every one of these roles, Nora has always followed God, and, in looking back, she discerns that God has also been following her. Her story helps us see the people and events of our lives in a new way—like lights that shine out in the darkness, revealing the certain path we have been on all along."

Anne Edwards, MSW, *Social Services Administrator*

"Nora takes us on a rich spiritual journey that abounds with the warmth and heart of a person who is clearly a great woman of faith, gifted mother, and charismatic woman leader. She tells stories from her life that provide us with deep insights. I feel that *Spiritual Connections* is a must read in these uncertain times of global and personal crises, divides and disconnects. Nora leaves us with a sense of hope and renewed vision to navigate these challenging days."

Angelika Selle,
President, Womens Federation for World Peace, USA

Acknowledgements

I wish to express my heartfelt gratitude to all those who have offered valuable input into this work. To Anne Edwards for her thoughtful editorial expertise and to Jonathan Gullery for designing and preparing this manuscript for publication. To Farley and Betsy Jones, Edwin and Marie Ang and David and Takeko Hose for helping me remember the path that we walked together.

To my parents who have given me a spiritual heritage and foundation with roots to stand and with wings to fly, and to my eight siblings whose love I cherish. To my husband Hugh who shares this story with me and who provided extensive research into events and dates as well as constant love and support. To our children, Andrea, Christopher, Ameri and High-Linn, who have enriched our lives with their creativity and love.

Preface

Life is a series of connections. As water moves continuously throughout the world, tying all of us together in its ebb and flow, and as air moves in and out of our bodies and all around us in the atmosphere, likewise a universal energy flows among us, connecting us to our Creator. Some call this energy Prime Force, Chi, or the Holy Spirit. Whatever it is called, it connects us to God and gives us life.

This life energy is like the current that flows through a string of lights on a Christmas tree. Some experiences stand out like sparkling lights, but behind them is the flow of invisible energy that connects them all. Throughout my life, as certain events have occurred, an awareness of this connecting energy has given my life meaning, purpose, and ultimate fulfillment.

In contemplating a theme and title for this memoir, the word "Connections" seemed to catch my thoughts on many levels. First, there is the connection to God. In addition, I always felt like I was "connecting" people—to each other—to jobs and careers—to resources that filled their needs—to angels—to ideas. Therefore, I chose *Spiritual Connections* as the title for this manuscript.

During the process of writing I browsed through an album of letters and photos presented to me for my 70th birthday and came across a letter written by a friend, Sharon. She wrote:

Nora often called herself a facilitator, a matchmaker. To me, Nora is a "connector"! . . . My soul has found its work; which I love with a passion! All of this has its roots in the connecting thread that points back to Nora, my "angel of connection"! Thank you for fine-tuning the "heart connection" for us all.

In re-reading this, I thank Sharon for her compliment and for highlighting the book title.

CHAPTER 1

Roots and Wings

I found faith, strength, and love in stories of my ancestors, and I was born into a family and community that had the same attributes. In the history of my Swiss Anabaptist ancestors and in the traditions of my Pennsylvania Mennonite family, I found roots to keep me grounded and wings to fly far—into uncharted territory.

Freedom in America

In the early 1700s, Christian, an Anabaptist minister, moved with his family from Switzerland to Germany to escape religious persecution. The German government, which initially exempted the non-violent Anabaptists from military service, had reneged on its promise when faced with the European wars. The family began seeking another refuge, this time in America. Members of their congregation had already begun immigrating to Pennsylvania, where William Penn promised universal religious freedom on his land grant.

Christian was my seventh great-grandfather. He and his wife, Elizabeth, and their seven children were ready. They had sold their belongings and packed the essentials for life in the new world. A week before they were to leave, tragedy struck.

Take the Children and Go

While chopping wood, Christian got a splinter in his hand resulting in blood poisoning, and just days later, he died. On his deathbed, he told Elizabeth, "Take the children and go to America. You will never have religious freedom here." The new widow summoned the courage to bring seven children on a challenging voyage to America. Upon their arrival in Pennsylvania, they were welcomed by members of the congregation who had left Germany earlier. This group had bought farmland about sixty miles west of Philadelphia and had already established a church.

Their fellow parishioners took the family to the fertile lands of Lancaster County, Pennsylvania. A family friend, Hans Groff, divided his farm and gave them a section of land to start their own farm. The church community built a house and barn for the family, and Elizabeth and her eldest son began farming.

My sixth great grandfather, the youngest child of Christian and Elizabeth, also named Christian, was ten years old when they arrived in America. He would later become a well-loved minister and bishop in the church. He authored a widely-translated book in German, called *Confessions of Faith*, which is still used to instruct new members of the church. Hans Groff would also become my ancestor when his daughter married the younger Christian. This family were among other ancestors from the same group who came to Lancaster County from Germany between 1720 and 1735.

My eyes fill with tears of gratitude when I think of my seventh great grandmother, Elizabeth, and what she endured to establish our family in America. She and members of her community worked hard to build an abiding church, productive farms, and stable families in the Lancaster area.

I feel a strong connection to my heritage. My heart is full when I think of the great thinkers, political leaders, people of faith, and hardworking families who responded to God's call to build a nation for worldwide seekers of freedom.

My Large Family

For generations, Mennonite families have thrived as farmers of fertile lands in America. Their large families supported one another, and Sunday afternoons saw the early settlers—cousins, aunts, uncles, and church friends—visiting each other's farms. Generations later, these traditions continued. My own childhood was filled with similar visits, giving me joyous memories and a deep sense of peace and freedom. My siblings and I roamed the gentle, rolling hills, fed and watched the animals grow, cared for the lush gardens of vegetables, and picked fruit from the trees.

Our family when I was 14 years old with 8 of the 9 children.
I am on the far right.

As the eldest of nine children, I had a special connection with my busy parents, and they often took me into their confidence. They did this with love, while letting me know that my position in the family meant that I should be a responsible example for my younger siblings. My mother taught me much about caring for a home and family, always with the serious expectation that I would be an exemplary child. My father, who was more relaxed, made learning fun.

An aerial view of our farm. Cattle are grazing in the pasture.
A three story chicken house extends behind the house.

Living on a farm meant both my parents were always there, so our family worked, played, and worshiped together. My father started out as a dairy farmer, but we later moved to a new farm where he built a large poultry house. We children gathered eggs, graded them, and packed them for market. If we dropped a basket, my mother made lots of egg noodles and angel food cake! When my mother was canning and freezing vegetables or fruits from our garden, everyone helped. When my father was harvesting the crops and needed extra help, we all pitched in. We were always together.

Close Calls

I was four years old, and my brother Lloyd was two. We had a baby sister, so my mother sent us to be with my father as he did farm chores. On the second level of the barn in the hayloft, there was a hole in the floor through which my father passed bales of hay to feed the cattle in the stalls below. As Lloyd and I ran around playing, my father called out to me: "Nora, watch that Lloyd doesn't get too close to the hole." I watched him as we played, but suddenly he was gone! My brother had fallen through the hole to the cement floor below.

I felt shock and fear walking behind my father as he carried my brother's limp body over his shoulder to the house. Lloyd had a concussion. He soon recovered, but the feeling that I had failed my duty stayed with me. This was the first of many times that I felt responsible for others, and this sense became a strong part of my personality. Being the eldest child in a family of nine children was instrumental in my later decision to be a social worker.

Working on a farm carries the risk of accidents, and I had my own narrow escape when I was five. We had just finished dinner when Titus, our farm hand, rose from the table and announced, "I am going out to fill my car with gas." We had a gas tank and pump on the farm. I followed close behind and watched as he slowly backed up his car to align it with the gas pump. Suddenly, somehow I found myself under the car, lying flat on my stomach, watching the front wheels, and trying to stay in the middle to avoid them. I started to cry, not because I was hurt but because I was scared.

Titus stopped the car, jumped out, and watched me crawl out from under it with only scratches on my knees. My parents said that when Titus brought me to the house he was as white as a sheet! How I got under a moving car without being hurt, I will never know, but it gave me a beginning sense that God had placed me on earth for a purpose.

A Budding Seeker

Even as a child, I had an innate sense of spirituality. I was curious, and from an early age sought answers to many questions. In our home, we had no television or radio, but I read every printed word I could get my hands on. I remember reading *The Scarlet Letter* when I was a bit too innocent to figure out what the sin was!

My closest friend in elementary and middle school was Roman Catholic. In a school where most kids shared similar beliefs, we were different, and we discussed our religious and lifestyle differences with great interest. We often compared our faiths. The nuns' habits had much in common with the modest dress of Mennonites, but my parents' church would not have accepted many of the liturgical rites of the Catholic Church.

Once I asked my mother, "Mom, do you think the Mennonites are the only ones who are right? What if the Catholics who think they have the true church are right? How do we know?" My ten-year-old mind was curious, but I am sure my mother was surprised. I cannot remember what she answered, but I do remember the question.

Special Projects with My Mother

My mother had a busy schedule caring for her family, and she did much of the shopping by mail order from the *Sears, Roebuck and Co. Catalog*. When I was in second or third grade, we ordered valentine cards for me to give out to my classmates. As Valentine's Day drew near, I watched daily for the mail carrier to bring the package. Finally, on the last possible delivery day, there was still no package! My little heart was broken.

Seeing my disappointment, my mother said, "Okay, get the crayons, scissors, and paper. We are going to make some valentine cards, and we will use some old ones as patterns." We spent the whole evening tracing, coloring, and cutting out valentines. The next day, feeling satisfied, I gave each of my classmates a homemade card. They may not have appreciated the effort my mother made, but I did.

Forgiveness Instead of Permission

We were a creative family, and my mother liked the finer arts. My father was creative with his hands, and he often worked in his workshop in the garage. As kids, we were always making things.

We had never had a Christmas tree. Christmas was to honor Jesus, and a decorated tree was considered secular. One Sunday afternoon before Christmas, while my parents were out, we children cut down a tree in the meadow. We brought it into the house and decorated it with paper ornaments. When my parents came home, they didn't have the heart to destroy it, so they moved it to the storage room where we could go to admire it. Of course, it was hidden from public view!

Building with My Father

When I was seventeen, my father built a new addition to our house. After drawing the plans, he began the building process that summer. Showing me the plans, he said, "Nora, I'm going to teach you every step in building a house." I learned to lay bricks and blocks, do electrical work, and use the table saw. I was intrigued by learning to make special finishes like mitered edges. We did everything together, and, when autumn rolled around, our new addition was complete. I am grateful for the training that makes me the handyman of the house today!

Time to Think

Living on the farm with our large family strengthened our connection to each other and to nature. It also gave me the opportunity to develop a deep-rooted faith in God. With no television, movies, or even radio, there was time to think. I loved being outdoors, and there I contemplated life. Watching the soft white clouds drifting by and taking different forms, my thoughts also took form. "Who am I?" I wondered. "Where is the seat of my identity?"

I knew I was creative and artistic, so I asked the universe, "Where did my abilities come from?" I wondered if the ability to draw and create was in my mind or in my hands. "It must be in my mind," I concluded, "so my identity must be in my mind." I recorded some of this thinking in a journal that I called *"Golden Threads."* Threads! I was already thinking about connections. I was also enjoying the process of writing. A favorite place to write was sitting in an apple tree overlooking the cattle grazing in the meadow. It was a sweet and gentle time.

A Year of Awakening

The age of twelve seems to be the age when something awakens in the mind and heart, and this was true for me. I had a sixth-grade teacher who often challenged my thinking. One night I had a dream in which he told me, "You will become famous." I remembered this simple dream and recalled thinking, "Me, a humble, little Mennonite farm girl; that's not very likely!" At the same time, my sense of purpose was growing.

Around this age, I had two realizations that gave me direction in the journey toward adulthood. Observing those around me, I became aware that people were often afraid of each other. I was shy myself and often avoided approaching people. I noticed others were as fearful of approaching me as I was of approaching them! When I pondered this idea, it seemed that no one else realized this. I knew this secret, so I must reach out to others and make them feel comfortable. I became determined to approach people first.

Soon I discovered that adults, even important people, responded. They seemed happy to have my acceptance. This was the secret of life, the secret of joy, the secret of relationships! Before this discovery, I cast my eyes down as I walked to school and even walked on the other side of the street to avoid saying "Hello." Now I deliberately sought out people to greet, especially if they looked sad or shy. With a new sense of freedom, I noticed that people sought me out as well.

The second realization was that people respect the genuine person rather than a façade that doesn't necessarily have internal value. I saw that adults sometimes tried to appear smart, knowledgeable, beautiful, or wealthy, yet I also observed that people loved the genuine person rather than these embellishments. At this early age, I understood there was no reason for me to be shy around even the greatest of people. Emboldened by a sense of power from within, I approached life with a new confidence.

Embracing Differences

Emerging from the Anabaptist movement, the Mennonites believed that a person should be baptized only when old enough to make a mature confession of faith. I made the commitment to join the church, and to be baptized when I was seventeen. I took this very seriously, even though part of me felt such a decision might limit my expression of faith, for I was making a committment to a very defined lifestyle.

As a Mennonite, I dressed according to our community traditions. Our faith stressed simplicity and humility, so I did not cut my hair, and I wore a small white cap, called a "prayer covering." I wore simple dresses that my mother made. Later I began to sew and enjoyed making clothes for my younger sisters and myself. I am sure there are times when every Mennonite girl dreams of wearing fancy clothes like everyone else. One does not dress differently without calling attention to the difference.

As a child, I accepted our way of dressing as a part of our Mennonite faith. Since life was good, stable, and secure, I did not rebel. Later, I learned that some Mennonites who had left the community for a broader lifestyle felt socially deprived and sometimes embarrassed by the simplicity of their heritage. This realization added to my understanding of the value of being genuine and not to pretend I was something that I wasn't. This became a pattern for my life.

Years later, as a graduate student at New York University, I would be, for the first time, immersed in a non-Mennonite environment. My earlier decision to be myself helped me to see my heritage of being simple, humble, and religious as a thing of beauty; a strength that I found lacking in the world around me. I was in the world at large, but "No, I did not know how to dance, and no, I did not know what a Bloody Mary was, because I had never tasted alcohol." Conversations often centered on current movies, TV shows, singers, or entertainment, about which I knew nothing. I could either pretend to know about them, be embarrassed about not knowing, or respond that these things had not been part of my life. I chose to tell them how it was. Somehow, this piqued their curiosity, and fascinating conversations could emerge about deeper issues. Soon I discovered people invited me to parties because I was "interesting."

Out-of-the-Box Job Possibility

Years before my New York University experience, I was eighteen years old and ready to work outside of my home. A classified advertisement in our local newspaper described an opening for a fashion designer, and it caught my attention. Of course, I wore plain clothes of a simple style, but I was artistic and often drew designs. I could design my own clothes and sew well. I was also adept at making patterns.

I asked my parents if I could apply for this job, and after discussing my request, they decided I could. My father drove me to Lancaster for the interview. I felt excitement, mixed with trepidation, as I approached the office in my homemade dress with simple neckline details. Somehow, I convinced the interviewer that I could design and make patterns, and one week later, I received a letter offering me the job. My surprised parents must have thought it unlikely I would get the job offer. They advised me not to take it, and I accepted their advice.

Looking back, I am grateful to them for letting me try, and I'm also glad they steered me away from a secular career at that time in my life. Instead, I worked as a cashier at the local grocery store.

Opening the Mind's Doors

High school was a concern for my church community. Being curious about the world and everything in it, I had loved every minute of school, but by the time I had completed my first year of high school, I was faced with one of my first great struggles. My parents and our conservative church believed that higher education could corrupt our simple faith; so like my church friends and relatives, I quit school to take on domestic duties at home to support our large family. Our tradition was that the girls worked in the house and the boys on the farm to help our parents until we were twenty-one years of age. If we had not married at that point, then we could pursue our own life goals. Although I had dated, the thought of marriage at that time felt confining. I felt I might be stuck in a smaller world than my mind envisioned.

Deep in my heart, I longed for more education, so I decided to go to college! Upon turning the magic age of twenty-one, I went to my former high school principal and asked to borrow the textbooks required for the remaining three years of high school. Returning home with a box full of books, including two years' worth of Latin textbooks, I began studying to finish high school.

Making myself a schedule, I studied from four to five o'clock each morning before going to work at my job in a local sewing factory. After three months, I decided to take the first set of GED tests at a local college. After examining the schedule, I noticed the tests were given over a three-day period. I decided to sign up to take many of the tests, even though I had not studied for all of them. To my surprise, I passed them all! Except for Latin credits, I had completed high school in three months. Adding one more year of self-study, I gained two years of Latin credits and completed the requirements for my high school diploma.

I was grateful for my family and for everything I had learned growing up on the farm. Life in my Mennonite community gave me a wonderful heritage, made rich with tradition, sacrifice, faith, and love. Looking back, I can see that my early life gave me a solid runway from which to take off. Now, I was ready to fly.

All 9 of the children in our family when I was 25 years of age.
I am on the left.

CHAPTER 2

Higher Education

I did not know exactly what my next steps would be, but I knew I wanted more education. I was thirsty for knowledge, skills, and abilities I would need for a career, and for life experiences beyond those I had growing up. I also knew that my connection to God would be the guiding light for all the decisions I made.

Two-Year Transition

With high school diploma in hand, I was almost ready for college, but not quite. Before enrolling, I needed some experience in the outside world, away from my tight-knit community. In October 1960, I entered Mennonite Voluntary Service, a program sponsored by a less conservative Mennonite Church, and I chose a project that involved working with children of migrant workers in Homestead, Florida.

Our team of eleven volunteers cared for preschool children while their parents labored in the fields. We worked and played hard together. I had already considered becoming a social worker, and this exposure to life beyond my childhood home furthered that interest. I learned that I cared about people and their emotional, social, and economic well-being. My work with Mennonite Voluntary Service provided my first real exposure to poverty and to interacting with other cultures.

As a transition from the cocoon of my youth to a broader adulthood, the two years of voluntary service was important for my social development. The migratory workers from the Appalachian Mountains were a lively bunch. They sang and played guitars, laughed, and joked. Many had their own form of foot-stomping and hallelujah-shouting Christianity. It was quite a contrast with my reserved form of worship and more contemplative lifestyle. Having been accustomed to singing hymns acapella and praying silently, I found that in this atmosphere my connection with God sparkled with greater spirit. I learned to express my love for God and Jesus in a more dynamic way.

College: a Bigger World

In 1962 with invigorated faith, I headed for college in the beautiful Shenandoah Valley in Virginia. Students at Eastern Mennonite College, now Eastern Mennonite University, shared my religious background, but most of them were less conservative than my community of Weaverland Conference Mennonites. Life at EMC opened my mind to new ideas, and the flow of knowledge there helped me put my simple early experiences into a larger context. What had been my whole world was now part of the world at large.

Two of my favorite courses were Philosophical and Intellectual History of Europe and the History of Christianity. My college years would offer a wealth of intellectual stimulation, but that was not all. At EMC, I was introduced to a variety of Mennonite branches and learned more about missionary work and world service projects. Every Sunday, I joined a team of students who visited homes to be of service to the mountain folks of Appalachia. In classrooms and in service work, our common faith made it comfortable and easy to study and work with my classmates.

Spiritual Fire

Sometimes we outgrow our worldview or religious understanding and begin to feel disillusioned. I have always been thankful that whenever I was on the verge of such disconnection, God opened a new door in my heart and brought my life into a larger religious experience, a new spiritual flow.

Change can require letting go of the old and taking a leap of faith into the new—an experience which is never comfortable or easy, as neither the old nor the new supports the leap. In my senior year at EMC, I experienced God in a way that had a powerful impact on my spiritual journey.

In the early 1960s, a spiritual fire had started at Yale University. Five college students who were praying together began to experience gifts of the spirit such as speaking in tongues, as described in the Bible in I Corinthians 12-14. They shared these Pentecostal type experiences of the Holy Spirit with students on other campuses, and the charismatic movement spread like wildfire! Throughout the country, college students were speaking in tongues and receiving other gifts of the spirit. At that time, this fire from the Holy Spirit touched congregants in Protestant and Roman Catholic denominations alike, challenging Christians to embrace a more dynamic expression of their faith.

One day I saw an announcement on the bulletin board at the EMC student center. It was an invitation for students to attend a speech by a student from another university on this spirit-filled charismatic experience. My roommate, Susan, and I decided to attend.

In the meeting room at the student center, there was electricity in the air. With great interest, I listened to the presentation about the work of the Holy Spirit empowering students on campuses throughout the country. As the speaker shared his own experiences, Susan became anxious and whispered to me, "This is Satan. I cannot be involved with this," nevertheless we continued to listen. At the end of the speech, an invitation was given for those who were interested in receiving the Holy Spirit to remain in the room. With Susan and others in the audience, I left and met outside with friends who were discussing the meeting.

I had left the room, but in fact God had touched my heart and mind. I said to my friends, "I feel like I just said no to God." I was conscious that this was not a mainstream experience, and as a resident advisor, I felt responsible for the spiritual life of those in my section of the dorm. Therefore, we decided I should return to the meeting and my friends would go to their rooms and pray for me.

Walking back to the student center, I opened the door where a joyful noise greeted me. Students were sitting in a circle, and some were speaking in tongues. Others were saying, "Hallelujah!" Feeling a bit overwhelmed, I sat down just inside the door and outside the circle, wondering what to do next. I did not have to wait long. My mouth immediately flew open. I could not keep it shut. A flow of words came forth like the pouring out of my heart in a heavenly language. I couldn't stop. Someone came over, praising God and inviting me into the circle of praying students. I was about to begin a more vibrant and joyful walk with God.

When I returned to my dormitory room, Susan greeted me at the door with tears streaming down her face. She said, "Nora, I know it happened to you. It happened to me too! When I got back here, I told God I was willing to let go of everything, including my fiancé, and suddenly I began to speak in tongues."

From that point on, my mind felt so clear I barely needed to study. At the same time, studies seemed less demanding, and exams seemed easier. I had a greater awareness that my life was connected to the spiritual energy that flowed throughout the universe! It was like tapping into a higher spiritual dimension than I had known before. When I read the Bible, the words seemed like they were on fire! I began to see Biblical truth more clearly. I was living a more energized spiritual life, accompanied by a deeper understanding. As a group, those of us who shared this experience spent many evenings together in prayer meetings. Life was full to overflowing, and I was so grateful to God and Jesus for leading me to this powerful new experience.

Through all the years since then, I have known with certainty that God is leading me on a path of light, even in times of struggle. The new level of enlightenment that blessed me through my charismatic experiences has never left me.

Graduate School in the Big Apple

I completed college in three years and two summers, graduating in 1965 with a degree in sociology. Having been accepted to two graduate schools, it was time to decide between them and move on. I obtained grants and full scholarships to the schools of social work at the University of Pennsylvania and New York University. Believing there was a plan for my life, I chose NYU because being in New York City would give me the greater stretch of experience in preparation for a career in social work or whatever God had in mind.

Living in a large city and attending graduate school with a diverse group of classmates would have its challenges, but I felt ready to embrace them. One big decision that loomed before me was whether to continue to dress like a Mennonite, especially by wearing the prayer covering on my head. Less conservative Mennonites wore it only to church. After much contemplation, I decided not to wear it because it would be an identifying feature of my person. I thought, "People will obviously ask me why I wear it, and unless I think everyone should wear one, why should I make it a part of my identity?" At first, I felt naked. I remember walking down the street thinking, "No one knows who I am. Nothing sets me apart." I continued to dress simply and modestly, in keeping with the values of my family and community, but I had taken a step away from the traditions of my youth.

Study at NYU broadened my understanding of human nature and relationships. I had one Jewish professor for whom I wrote many papers on personal growth. Sometimes he challenged me in class about my beliefs. Most of my colleagues were not overtly religious, so sometimes I felt put on the spot. Once he said he had a Zen Buddhist friend whose beliefs resonated with how I described my relationship with God. Later I came to believe that he had a sincere curiosity about my unique background and spiritual journey, but in the moment, I often felt singled out.

My Family in New York City

Going to a movie theater was not acceptable for my family, nor was having a TV in our home. I had viewed educational films in college, but a full-length movie for entertainment had not been part of my life. When I arrived for graduate school in New York City, one of my goals in becoming educated was to go to a movie. I chose *Sound of Music* as the first one. What a heart opener! I loved it! I thought I must have missed many great experiences, but after *that* movie, every other one was a disappointment.

I longed to share this movie with my family, so I invited my two youngest sisters, Margaret and Joyce, ages twelve and eight respectively, to visit me in the big city. As part of an excursion, I took them to see *Sound of Music,* explaining they could tell our parents that they had seen a film. They loved it and memorized the songs. I later heard that our house and meadows rang out with the joyful songs from the movie as my sisters danced and sang. I did not feel I had corrupted them but exposed them to the kind of beauty that only God could have inspired!

New York City opened doors to an urban world and new experiences. This was my first exposure to a non-Mennonite environment.

I also invited my parents to visit me in Manhattan, hoping to take them on their first subway ride and show them the sights of the city. To my dismay, on the day they came, the city announced a public transportation strike. I could not take them anywhere. I remember my father sitting in my dormitory room, looking out the window at the traffic on Fifth Avenue, and I was disappointed to think how boring this must be for my farmer father. Fortunately, one of my friends had a car and took us around the city for a day. I had wanted my parents to experience the excitement of the city, but instead, they probably went back to their farm and greeted it with joyful relief!

As I neared the end of my formal education, I asked God to show me the next step. I had no debt and no attachments that would keep me from going anywhere in the world. "Where will that be?" I asked. "Should it be a mission?"

How could I know that God was waiting in the wings with an answer?

A Providential Encounter

My introduction to the Unification Church, then known in America as the Unified Family, began at Columbia University in New York City, where I was speaking at a forum sponsored by a group called Youth for Christ. The topic was "With Heart and Mind," and I was speaking on the heart side of the Christian experience.

From the stage, I noticed two girls in the audience, seated apart, with whom I felt an affinity. After the speech, I met them both. Their names were Barbara and Diane, and they told me about a group they were part of, the Unified Family, where I could come to hear a series of lectures based on a teaching called the Divine Principle. I told them I was writing my master's thesis on *The Extent to Which Values Learned in Childhood Change in Adulthood*, and I was seeking groups I could interview for my research. I was interested in their teachings, and they invited me to hear the lectures at their apartment on 44th Street.

At this time, the movement was called the Unified Family, reflective of the mission to bring all of humankind to our home with our heavenly parent, God. The more official "Unification Church" name was adopted later.

After meeting Barbara and Diane, I went to their apartment every Tuesday evening to hear lectures on the Divine Principle. Upon arriving for the first time, I met Myrtle, an older woman, who said, "I saw you last night." I had been downtown to see a movie at the Newman Center, and I looked at her in amazement. How could she remember a stranger she saw in New York City?

Later she said she had noticed me and wanted to invite me to hear the lectures but changed her mind because I looked like I was happy with my life and not searching for anything new. It seemed God had decided I should meet the Unification Church one way or the other!

The apartment where the lectures were taught was small and simply furnished. The first thing I noticed was a large blackboard on the living room wall that to me stood out like a sore thumb, but for Barbara and Diane, it was essential to their mission of sharing a special revelation. After I was seated in front of this chalkboard, Barbara eagerly began to share the teachings.

A Comprehensive Worldview

The first lecture, called the Principle of Creation, taught that God, as Creator, was the source of both male and female attributes, and human beings were created to reflect this. Man and woman together were to establish a family unit within the larger family of humankind centered on God, our heavenly parent. All creation was to be brought into this relationship with God, creating the kingdom of heaven on earth and a world of peace.

They also taught about the spiritual dimension, explaining that each of us has an eternal spirit or soul that goes on living in the afterlife after the body dies. A clear description of the workings of this spiritual world satisfied many of my questions concerning the mystical aspect of earthly life. I was fascinated with the simple yet profound explanation of the relationship between God, humanity, and the creation.

The second lecture, called The Fall of Man, taught how the first couple deviated from God's beautiful plan of true love and created the family of humankind outside of God's direct lineage. This deviation from true love resonated with me as truth. I was studying psychology, and I understood that many problems of mental illness had roots in guilt that was often associated with the misuse of sex, including sexual abuse.

The lectures that followed also made sense to me. As our heavenly parent, God had to make a way to redeem his erring children and reconnect them to the heavenly lineage. Thus, Jesus was chosen to initiate the central lineage through which all of humankind could be reconnected to

God. Jesus came to establish the kingdom of heaven on earth by bringing the human family and the whole of creation back to God's original ideal.

When I first heard the Divine Principle, I already loved Jesus. The understanding that Jesus had come to create the kingdom of heaven on earth struck a chord with me, and I recognized it as true. The idea that *the end of the world* meant *the beginning of a new age* also caught my attention, as it was something I had already considered as a possibility.

The remaining lectures continued with an explanation of a path of restoration by showing parallels between different ages in biblical history. Because I had taken a course on the history of Christianity in college, I was familiar with the historical events being explained, and I was fascinated to see that they fell into repetitive historical patterns. Because of my charismatic experience, my beliefs were not dogmatic or fixed, and I was open to move onward and upward in my journey with God.

A Defining Step

It was exciting to realize that God was working at this time in history to bring about world peace and gather his family through a chosen person on earth, but it also gave me cause for concern and consideration. For four months, I prayed to know whether this was the right path. I perused commentaries on the book of Revelation seeking answers as to God's will for me. Like the disciples of Jesus who left their lives behind to follow God's chosen son, I had to grapple with this new understanding and take responsibility for my response to it. My heart resonated with the beautiful and lofty words of the Christian hymn *Higher Ground:*

I'm pressing on the upward way,
New heights I'm gaining every day;
Still praying as I'm onward bound,

"Lord, plant my feet on higher ground."
Lord, lift me up and let me stand,
By faith, on Heaven's tableland,
A higher plane than I have found;
Lord, plant my feet on higher ground.

To follow this path was not an easy decision. I did not make it lightly. When I said "yes", it was like my heart knew—and I felt great joy. I was joining a band of disciples who would change the world and bring humanity into God's family. I felt peace in accepting this truth but also felt a great responsibility for this understanding.

The Divine Principle had resonated with my heart and shed light on the deeper meaning of the universe, from the basic science of the atom to the mysteries of the spiritual world and life after death. The teachings were divine inspirations given to Sun Myung Moon, a man who had grown up in humble circumstances in war-torn North Korea. He had been imprisoned there before fleeing to South Korea where he continued to teach Christian seekers.

When Sun Myung Moon was fifteen years of age, Jesus appeared to him in a vision on a Korean mountainside on Easter morning in 1935. Jesus had expressed his anguish that he had not been able to establish the kingdom of heaven on earth and bring all of humankind into God's family. Although Jesus had sacrificed his life on the cross and paid the price for individual spiritual salvation, part of his work remained unfinished, and the children of earth still suffered from original sin. The kingdom of heaven and a world of peace were waiting for God's chosen person to undertake a great mission, and Jesus asked the teenaged Sun Myung Moon to do this. With great courage, sincere determination, and absolute sincerity, he received the baton from Jesus and began to seek answers that would guide him in reaching out to the world.

Subsequently, in his autobiography, *As a Peace-Loving Global Citizen*, he stated:

> *For years I have called for a world where all religions live together as one, all races live as one, and all nations exist as one. For thousands of years, history has seen the continuous increase of divisions. Each time a different religion was adopted or a new regime came into power more boundaries were drawn and wars were fought. Now, however, we live in an age of globalism. For the sake of the future we must become one.*

Yielding to God

While I was studying the Divine Principle, other students were also coming to the small apartment to hear the message. Neil, Farley, Helen, and I were hearing the lectures at the same time, and we often exchanged views and inspirations about the ideas we were contemplating. Ultimately, we all joined this small Unified Family, and our paths were to cross frequently. Farley and Neil both went on to become presidents of the Unification Church in America.

I heard the lectures while I was finishing my thesis and preparing to graduate from NYU. It was an exciting time, and my interest in completing my academic studies sometimes took a back seat to my study of the Divine Principle. I began to realize that my future would be a response to the profound, life-changing truth God had brought into my life.

After getting my GED at the age of twenty-one, my higher education had led to formal academic study and significant intellectual growth, a wider life experience, and most importantly, a higher understanding of God.

Through the Mennonite Volunteer Service Program, I learned about human problems and potential solutions. Through the charismatic movement, I had experienced the love and presence of God more fully within my heart and soul. Now, through the Divine Principle, I had found a greater understanding of God's ideal and his determination to realize one-ness with his children throughout human history. The teachings satisfied my intellectual curiosity as well as my longing for an ever-deeper relation-ship with the living God.

All of this was happening against the backdrop of living beyond the confines of my Mennonite community and gaining a broader under-standing of how the world works. Looking back, I can see that God was working closely with me to make sure I was getting a higher education on all levels—academic, practical, and spiritual! I believed I could trust myself to make a judgment because of all that I had experienced, but the decision to move forward required humility—a complete yielding of my life to God.

CHAPTER 3

School's Out! Tending Faith

I had accepted the Divine Principle teaching largely because it made sense to me based on what I had already experienced in my life of faith. Intuitively, I felt God was leading me to this understanding. I also encountered extraordinary people who were teaching and following this path. I felt a deep connection with some of them, and they were influential in helping me feel that this was God's plan for my life. During the next few years, I would build a new foundation of faith in a wider world.

First Spiritual Mentors

In June 1967, I became the grateful recipient of a master's degree in social work without having gone to high school. I had worked a long time for this accomplishment! Earlier in April, two months before I received my graduate degree, I signed a church membership form and moved into the New York Unified Family Church Center with Barbara and Diane, my spiritual mentors.

The first time I saw Barbara and Diane, I had felt a connection with them. Later I learned both of them had grown up as Quakers, or Friends, believing that everyone has the light of God within—a view that I shared. They were against war and placed a high value on social justice, as I did. They had attended a Friends school together, as young women of faith.

When they met the Unified Family, they had taken a giant leap to accept the Divine Principle. It was easy to view them as mentors because of their dedication, intelligence, and graceful way of living.

After graduation from NYU, I was ready for the next step.

Conforming to the strict routines that they practiced in the center was another matter altogether! Barbara and Diane had recently returned from six months of training with the Unification Church in Japan before opening a teaching center in New York. Modeling the New York center after the centers in Japan, they ran a tight ship. I chaffed at what seemed like an oppressive lifestyle. Although externally I was a disciplined person, internally I was an independent and free spirit who needed an opportunity to express myself. I had just left a community of liberal students at New York University. Life with Barbara and Diane could not have offered a sharper contrast!

My commitment and desire to serve was based on my relationship with a God of love, and my mentors were running the center in New York with a heavy emphasis on duty and obedience, which they had inherited from Japanese culture. One Sunday morning, we went to Holy Ground in Central Park to pray. Holy Ground was a special place that Father Moon, our founder, had designated as a place to pray and meditate. As we prepared for our jaunt through the city, Diane announced, "We will do a silence condition on the way." Prayerfully, we made our way to the subway station, took the rackety train to Central Park, and walked in silence to the large rock that had been singled out and dedicated as Holy Ground. Surrounded by the noise of the city, it stood as a place to meet God.

Tension had already been building up in me, and this oppressive silence was the last straw. I was ready to explode! Walking to the top of the rock, I threw my arms in the air and shouted out to God, loudly pouring out my frustration and my need for full expression. Barbara and Diane looked on in shock. Afterwards, we talked and came to a better understanding of our different approaches and needs. I think all three of us grew as a result of that outburst.

Kingdom Building

Having completed my graduate work at NYU, there was no need for me to stay in New York City. I had made a commitment to the Unified Family and the Divine Principle, but I needed an answer to my next question: Where would I go? I needed to decide where I should work and live.

On an earlier visit to the Unification Church headquarters in Washington, D.C., I met Dr. Young Oon Kim, a Korean missionary who had brought the message of the Divine Principle to America. She was the guiding light for members at headquarters and at smaller residential centers around the country. When she suggested that I should consider moving to Washington for further training, I quickly agreed.

In August 1967, I moved into the Washington center. The church center at 1907 S Street was in a modest row house with a printing press in the basement, a living room, dining room, and kitchen on the main floor, and bedrooms on two additional floors above.

Most members who lived in the center worked full time or went to school and worked part time. I accepted a full-time job as a psychiatric social worker at St. Elizabeth's Hospital, where I worked in the outpatient department with a program of the National Institute of Mental Health. My grant for graduate study had included a commitment to work for two years in the field of psychiatric care.

Anne, another new member of the Unification Church, got a job at St. Elizabeth's as well, and we traveled together to work. We were both in our twenties, and we exchanged stories of our lives, discussed things that were going on in the center, and shared ideas. Sometimes, we prayed together after work, before going into the center. In the process, we became lifelong friends. Each evening, we joined the others in evangelical activities.

The twenty or more members who lived in the center were mostly young professionals who worked during the day and gave lectures in the evenings to a steady stream of inquiring guests. We also went out in groups hoping to meet interested people. Sometimes we worked together on newsletters, developed literature, and planned programs.

The early members lived, worked, studied, worshipped, and sang together. Some wrote beautiful songs, inspired by their new faith. Most members lived in the center, and we shared our earnings to support rent, food, utilities, and activities. Since I grew up in a large family, worked in a youth program in voluntary service, and lived in a college dormitory, communal living in a spiritual setting was appealing and comfortable for me.

Each member of the group was unique, but what we had in common was faith that a new world was coming. Whether we were cooking, cleaning, mending, working on a project, or witnessing to potential new members at coffee houses, church socials, or parks, we were family. I could sense the sincerity and faith of each individual and feel God's presence moving among us at group gatherings. My experience with Miss Kim and the members in Washington helped to confirm the decision that I had made.

The late 1960s in America was a time of change. Many young adults were seeking an alternative to their parents' lifestyle, which was often one of working nine-to-five and rising on the career ladder. Many youth were seeking answers to their concerns regarding the war in Vietnam, the sexual revolution, social justice, religious belief, and moral values. The concept that God was ushering in a new age centered on building a heavenly, peaceful kingdom on earth drew many a young seeker to our welcoming door.

A Song

At this point I will include the words of one of the many songs written by the members in the early days of our life in the church that catches the spirit of a movement of youth who are seeking to bring about the kingdom of heaven on earth. The following song was written by Dan Fefferman, a talented songwriter who wrote many powerful songs that capture the spirit and enthusiasm of the early years of our church in America:

As the day dawns out of the night
A generation will come forth
A generation of righteousness
Walking the way, the heavenly way of truth
Babylon! We've a message to send,
The resurrection is at hand!
And the generation of righteousness
Cometh now forth to heal the wounded land.
Ah, ah, ah, ah

For the dark will give way to the light,
And the race will rise out of the mud
And the generation of righteousness,
Will come forth shedding their tears, sweat and their blood,
And the blood of our God will pour forth o'er His own,
To make fertile a dry desert sand.
And he'll gather the fruit of the seeds He has sown.
Trampling vintage for the marriage of the lamb.
Ah, ah, ah, ah
God has given this land,
Claiming His right, winning His fight we stand.
You, who would build a new age,
Give me your hand, brother I know we can.
As the day dawns out of the night
A generation will come forth
A generation of righteousness
Walking the way, the heavenly way of truth

Miss Kim

Professor Young Oon Kim, whom we called Miss Kim, was the center of spiritual life and work at the headquarters. A serene tower of quiet strength and spiritual wisdom, she guided our daily lives, our worship experiences, and our spiritual development and growth. In America, she was the respected representative of Sun Myung Moon and his wife, Hak Ja Han Moon, and a link to their teachings and direction. Her impact on our lives was significant, and I owe much of my early life of faith in the Unification Church to her.

Miss Kim had come to know Jesus and follow Christianity as a teenager in Korea. Early in her Christian life, she came across the works of

Emmanuel Swedenborg who made real for her a deep understanding of the spiritual world.

Dr. Kim had been a professor at Ewha Womans University, the largest university for women in Korea and among the largest in the world. Prior to that, she had studied theology for five years at a seminary in Japan where she graduated with the highest academic honors. Later, she studied at a graduate school of theology at the University of Toronto in Canada. At those two seminaries, she had studied the history of Christian thought and considered a variety of interpretations of the Bible. Through all the years of academic study, a spark of divine love was always with her.

Dr. Young Oon Kim was a theological scholar from Korea who served as a mentor for the young members of the American movement.

In 1959, Miss Kim accepted the call to bring the Divine Principle to America. Once she arrived in the U.S., she consciously sought people who were dedicated, trustworthy, and capable of carrying out the mission. She translated the teaching of Father Moon into English in a style that would resonate well with a western audience.

Miss Kim taught that mastering human relationships is an essential key to a person's religious life and spiritual growth. She was a living example of how to love and follow the teachings with single-minded faith. She touched the lives of many members, enabling them to inherit her understanding and to incorporate the Divine Principle into their lives.

In the tradition of our Founders, Miss Kim sacrificed the foundation of the American church for the sake of the world by sending some of the earliest members in the USA to Germany, Austria, Italy, England, Spain, and Holland to pioneer the movement in Europe. Her path as a sincere Christian of stature lent credibility to the profound message she brought to America. This was true for me and others whose lives were rooted in the Christian faith.

As one of four missionaries from Korea, Miss Kim's role was to serve as a spiritual leader and advisor for American members. Soon after I moved into the center, she asked me to become the bookkeeper for our local center and the treasurer for the national headquarters of the church. I had never received training in bookkeeping, but I was honest and responsible, and I learned quickly. I was connected to the spiritual energy and work, but I was also a grounded, practical person. She may have realized that I needed a solid landing spot in my new life.

A Respected Scholar and New Friend

A week of leave from work during my first summer in Washington provided an opportunity for a new experience. Miss Kim suggested that we use our vacations to visit pioneer missionaries working in centers in other states, in order to offer encouragement. I used the time off work to visit Susan, a young girl who was a pioneer in Miami, Florida. During my one-week stay, Susan and I went out every evening to meet people.

One rainy evening, Susan suggested we attend a lecture by Dr. George Lamsa, a prominent Bible translator from the Middle East. After several bus transfers, we finally arrived at the church where he was speaking. The lecture was already in progress. Dr. Lamsa was an elderly gentleman, and most in the audience were elderly ladies who hung on his every word with obvious respect. I found myself fascinated with his insights.

Aramaic is the vernacular Middle Eastern language that Jesus and his disciples spoke. It made sense to me that those who first wrote the original New Testament texts had used their native language. Dr. Lamsa had translated the Bible directly from the oldest Aramaic texts into the English language.

Dr. Lamsa was born in an isolated Aramaic-speaking Christian community in Syria where the language and customs had remained static for over 2,000 years. With his knowledge and understanding of the life and times of Jesus, he brought to the Western world a deeper view of God's word as spoken by Jesus and the early Christians. He had devoted his life to recovering ancient documents, translating the Bible, and had written eighteen commentaries on the Bible.

Dr. Lamsa believed in the ecumenical Christian church and worked to create greater cooperation and understanding among Christians, Jews, and Muslims—all adherents to monotheistic religions with origins near the same area. He had once been hired by Roland V. Lee productions to be the technical director for the motion picture, *The Big Fisherman*. Oral Roberts had been so impressed with his Aramaic translation of the Bible that he printed a special Abundant Life edition for followers numbering in the tens of thousands.

Dr. Lamsa's explanations of idioms in the Bible were most interesting, and they resonated well with the teachings of the Divine Principle. After the meeting, I decided to invite him to speak to our Unified Family members in Washington. As I approached him, many of the audience members were crowded around him, but I finally reached him. When I did, he stopped, looked at me intently and said, "I wish you were my sister." Then he told me to write down my name and phone number and said he would get back to me. As he slipped this piece of paper into his coat pocket along with other items people gave him, I thought to myself, "This is the end of this contact." Nevertheless, his unusual comment stayed with me.

At the end of my one-week mission in Florida, I said goodbye to Susan and returned to Washington.

Invitation

The following week, I received a phone call from Dr. Lamsa's assistant, inviting me to a weekend retreat where he would be speaking in Bucks County, Pennsylvania. I was both surprised and pleased to receive the invitation. Maria, a member of our Washington church family, went with me to Pennsylvania, and we drove my VW for three hours to a lovely mountainside retreat.

Most of the guests were ministers who were eager to learn from Dr. Lamsa, but to my surprise, he singled me out again, asking me to sit by him at a table from which he was speaking and answering questions. The ministers looked up questioningly as I took my seat. When a break was announced, instead of mingling with other participants, he invited me to go with him on a walk around a nearby lake.

I am sure many of the ministers wanted to speak to Dr. Lamsa to ask him questions, but after each session, he continued to invite me to walk with him. I felt both honored and embarrassed to be taking up so much of his time. We talked about spiritual topics, and he was interested in my theological perspectives. Of course, I was interested in his. Ours had become a special spiritual connection.

Dr. Lamsa's Visit

After this three-day retreat, Dr. Lamsa accepted my invitation to visit our Unified Family center in Washington. He spent four days with us, speaking to our small group each evening. He explained Biblical passages and idioms in the context of the times and surroundings in which Jesus lived. His explanations regarding Jesus' life resonated with our Divine Principle teachings. For example, our understanding of the fall of man and Jesus' mission to build the kingdom of heaven on earth were similar to his interpretation of scripture. Dr. Kim thoroughly enjoyed discussions with him.

On October 14, 1969, I received a letter from Dr. Lamsa. He wrote, "I cannot tell you how happy I was to spend a week with the Unified Family. I enjoyed talking to your group." Years later, when my husband and I lived in Berkeley, California, he took us to meet an Eastern Church official who lived in exile in America. The Eastern Church arose in the area surrounding Palestine prior to the Eastern Orthodox Church. We also met when we were living in Kansas City, Missouri, and he was speaking there.

Dr. Lamsa and members of his Aramaic Bible Center felt a strong kinship with our Unification Church, and we kept in touch over the years. I still have the hand-written letters that Dr. Lamsa sent to me. I received a letter informing me that Dr. Lamsa had passed away on September 22, 2002, at the age of eighty-three. He had asked that I be notified when he died.

My relationship with Dr. Lamsa was a mystery to me, and I always wondered about the deeper meaning of our meeting. Someday I will understand. Knowing him was one of those light-filled connections that was deeper, more mysterious, and more spiritual than could be revealed on the surface. I always hoped our relationship brought a deeper understanding to him of what God was doing in the world today through our teachings. I also prayed that it could bring joy to this man on his lonely path of life-long service to God.

The Holy Bible

From

Ancient Eastern Manuscripts

One Christmas, I received from Dr. Lamsa a beautiful, leather-bound autographed Bible, which he had spent many years translating from Aramaic into English. This is an autographed copy.

Influential Connections

Barbara and Diane, various church members in New York and Washington, Young Oon Kim, and George Lamsa were important influences during my early years in the Unification Church. My connection with all of them strengthened my faith that God was guiding my steps. Dr. Lamsa didn't join our group, but he loved us. He felt drawn toward people who, like him, were serious, faithful, and focused on service to God and humanity. Like him, we had followed a path less traveled, and he recognized that we were kindred spirits.

CHAPTER 4

Love, Unification Church Style

The Divine Principle teaches that God longs to embrace all humanity as his direct descendants through the marriage blessing. As both father and mother of humankind, God is the source of the universal love energy that connects everyone on earth. At this moment in history, our Founders, whom we later called Father and Mother Moon, are viewed as the central couple through whom God is working to establish the kingdom of heaven on earth. Their mission is to extend God's marriage blessing to as many people as possible, so that each blessed couple can give birth to children born in the direct lineage of God. Such families are the essential building block of the kingdom of heaven on earth.

Our Founders arrive in America

In December 1968, as part of a world tour, Rev. and Mrs. Moon came to Washington. Our new center at 1611 Upshur St., NW was abuzz with excitement as we cleaned, prepared food, and spiritually aligned our hearts to greet this chosen couple through whom God was working to bring all humankind into one family under God.

Our Founders had a special reason for coming—to officiate the first Blessing Ceremony held in America. Even as Father Moon mingled with members who had come from all over the U.S. to meet him, he was thinking of potential couples. The atmosphere was filled with anticipation at our new headquarters located at 1611 Upshur Street, NW that was the venue for the ceremony.

The Reverend and Mrs. Moon

Our Founders had rooms on the second floor of Upshur House, and meetings with members who were blessing candidates were held there. Potential candidates from across the country waited to learn whether Father Moon had a match for them to consider. Miss Kim counseled some of us about potential marriage partners, and we had faith in her wisdom. We also believed that Father Moon had an intuitive ability to channel God's desire for our lifetime partners. One-by-one, couples emerged from an upstairs meeting room to the applause of their brothers and sisters, as we called one another.

Wedding Robes

With several other women, I became a member of the sewing committee to make twenty-six white robes, called holy robes, for thirteen couples. I remember scouring stores in the surrounding area for enough white taffe-ta-like fabric to meet this need, and we set up a little factory in the basement dining hall. While we were fitting robes on the brides, Father Moon stopped by to inspect our handiwork and said, "They are too short. They must drape completely to the floor over the shoes." My heart fell, as there was no time to remake them or find more fabric. We set about ripping out the hems, pressing out the seams, and sewing in false hems, thus adding one-and-a-half inches. I felt sorry that the wedding robes for these special couples were less than perfect, but it was what we could do. Best of all, it worked! The shoes were covered, and the robes met the standard that had been set.

First Blessing Ceremony in America

With the hurdle of the hem behind us, we prepared to enjoy the simple but beautiful and historic ceremony that would bring thirteen couples into their new position as blessed couples before God.

The Upshur Street headquarters had previously been the Libyan embassy. There was a certain elegance to the main entrance hall with its emerald-green carpet and winding stairway. Just off the main hall, the large connecting living rooms were lovingly decorated, and a banner was stretched across the front of the room. Music filled the air as members practiced entertainment for the occasion. The marriage ceremony was a sacred sacrament held in highest esteem by our members, and each person was prayerfully doing their best to make it a meaningful experience for everyone.

On February 28, the moment came when thirteen brides and grooms entered the room, bowing as they approached the altar where our Founders stood ready to welcome them into a growing circle of blessed families. These first thirteen couples in America represented the mission of our Founders to bring peace in the world by blessing couples who would embrace a larger circle in their marriages. There were two mixed-race couples, one with an African American partner and another with an Asian spouse. Other couples represented differences that were less obvious, but each one was making a foundation for a future world of peace, centered on God.

Leaving the Comfort Zone

In the spring of 1970, Miss Kim called together members of our growing headquarters center and announced that it was time for us to consider going out to spread the word across America. This meant moving to new, emerging centers throughout the country where small pockets of members were doing evangelical work.

I was one of four members who volunteered to work in another city, and I was assigned to Kansas City, Missouri. With both anticipation and a little sadness, I quit my job, packed my Volkswagen, and headed west. I had come to deeply love Dr. Kim and my fellow "fishers of men" in Washington. Now I would share my experiences in a new area. Arriving in Kansas City, I joined Dee and a small group of members who lived in a humble house with, of course, a large chalkboard in the living room, which was the trademark of a Unification Church center. I took a job at a Veterans Administration hospital, and with a team of mental health workers, helped to establish a daycare program for veterans living in the community. As I had done in Washington, I worked during the day and gave Divine Principle lectures on weekends and in the evenings.

Engagement

Shortly after my move to Kansas City, an announcement came from headquarters that an international marriage blessing would be held in Korea in October 1970. This was to be a blessing of 777 couples, and American couples were to be included. In July, I received a letter from Miss Kim saying that she was coming to visit us in Kansas City. My friend, Giovanni, who was working in the Unification Church center in St. Louis, Missouri, and I met to discuss her visit. We wanted to be prepared if she was coming to discuss matches for the blessing in Korea. We prayed about this, and I was inspired with two names. I felt this inspiration had come from God.

We were right. Miss Kim had traveled to meet with us about the blessing to be held in Korea! Upon her arrival, she told me that Father Moon had proposed a match for me, but when she stopped in California to meet with that person she discovered that he had left the church just that morning. "Maybe this is God's will," she said. Then she asked, "Do you have anyone in mind that I should present to Father Moon for you?"

The photo I submitted for the Blessing application

The first name I had received was the person who had just left the church, so I told her about the second person, Hugh Spurgin. Hugh and I had often been team partners, and we had worked together well. In fact, I had taught him part of the Divine Principle. Hugh was younger than I, and I was concerned that he may not be interested in being blessed with someone six years older than he, but I also knew there was a positive connection between us.

Dr. Kim returned to Washington and spoke with Hugh. On that very day, my name had been running through his mind. When she spoke to him, he immediately said yes. Hugh called me right away, sounding excited and very happy. But I was hesitant, wanting to be sure that he was okay with the difference in our ages, since I am six years older than Hugh is. Finally, he said, "Nora, I really want this, and I hope you do too." That was all that I needed to hear. Dr. Kim presented our names and photos to Father Moon who responded that we were a good match and would be a good couple. Thus began a new chapter in my life. Hugh and I were engaged.

Soon after our phone conversation, I received a letter from Hugh. Here is an excerpt:

> I've been a bit love sick but am slowly adjusting to the fact that we're to be blessed in October.… Don't worry about the differences in our ages. If we truly seek to become one—a God-centered pair—then nothing external matters And I have a strong feeling that the two of us are going to create a good life together and do and be things that I know I could only do with and for you. Even as I write, I feel freer to openly express myself and to make such commitments.

When we shared our news with both sets of parents, they were surprised at the sudden announcement but happy for us. My mother commented that he looked like a nice, clean-cut young man.

Courtship, Our Way

When Dr. Kim spoke with Hugh, he had just quit his U.S. government job and was preparing to go to Cleveland to start a new center. With this new development, Dr. Kim sent him instead to Kansas City; there we prepared spiritually for the blessing to be held several months later.

In our church, men and women did not date. We practiced abstinence until we received God's blessing. For Hugh and me, our time together before the blessing was deeply spiritual, and we felt the presence of God with us. As we shared our ideas and worked on the mission, we got to know each other better. Praying together at the end of each day strengthened our connection with God and with each other.

A Stop in Japan

On August 31, 1970, Hugh and I were among seven American couples who travelled to Japan for three weeks before going to Korea for the marriage blessing of 777 couples. Upon our arrival in Japan, my luggage did not arrive and I spent an entire week before it finally caught up with me. But there was work to do.

Speaking to groups in Tokyo from on top of a mini-van

We joined our Japanese brothers and sisters in giving anti-Communist speeches from atop a minivan—a unique experience for us! Driving around Tokyo together, we all memorized short speeches in Japanese to call through the loudspeakers on top of our van: "Nihon no minasima; konichiwa!" We addressed the Japanese audiences who gathered around our minivan to invite them to the World Anti-Communist League Rally on September 8.

It was a time when Communist students were quite active in Japan. As Americans, we brought a new energy to the anti-communist campaign of the hard-working Japanese members. In addition, we visited church centers in several cities, where energetic Japanese youth lived and taught the Divine Principle. Theirs was a young and thriving movement, and we learned much from them. Many of them were to join us in October for the Blessing Ceremony in Seoul.

Korea

When we arrived in South Korea, we heard moving testimonies from early Korean members who had followed Father Moon from the very beginning as he established a new religious movement in war-torn, poverty-stricken Korea. Many of them had been devout, spirit-filled Christians in North Korea who had received revelations that they should prepare for Jesus' return. Some early members had been university students who left their studies to witness for the church and teach the Divine Principle. Our own Dr. Young Oon Kim had been one of their professors.

We stayed at the church's training center at Sutaek-Ri in Gurii City on the outskirts of Seoul near the Il Hwa ginseng tea factory owned by our church. European blessing candidates soon joined us. In 1970, South Korea was a nation in great poverty. Some streets in Seoul were unpaved—with sewage running down dirt roads. The sight of sides of beef hanging outside of butcher shops stays with me. At the time, the contrast between the standards of living in our two nations was striking. Of course, since then, South Korea has realized dramatic economic growth.

Advice from Father Moon

Just days before the blessing ceremony, we were called to gather and prepare for personal interviews with Father Moon. Each of us was interviewed separately. I walked into the small room and was greeted by Father Moon who was sitting at a low table with our applications and photos before him. Mrs. Won Pak Choi, his assistant and interpreter, was there as well. He looked at both of our photos, looked up at me, and said, "You have a round face and a balanced nature." He then studied Hugh's face. "He is a pure man. That is rare among American men." Then he advised me, "You must keep his love. If it is lost, it would be hard to regain." He looked at our faces again and said we were a good couple who complemented each other well. With that, I was dismissed, and Hugh was invited into the room.

What a precious experience to be given marriage advice by this channel of God's love. I felt confident about our marriage, and I was determined to make ours a loving relationship so that we would never lose our love for one another.

Father Moon did not shy away from differences when matching a couple. For him, a wide gap offered a greater opportunity for growth and love. Once a gap was bridged, a couple could embrace an ever-expanding range of experiences and relate to a broader circle of people.

Hugh would be a faithful companion, and our relationship grew into a beautiful, solid marriage. We worked together to live a life of service to God and others, we gained inspiration and strength from each other to lead many projects and people, and we raised four wonderful children.

Holy Wine Ceremony

On one occasion, several days after arriving in Korea, we were awakened in the middle of the night and told to prepare to receive the holy wine. The European and American couples gathered to await this special ceremony. Lining up in a room just large enough for all of us, each couple received a small cup of holy wine from which each partner drank one-half. This very sacred ceremony symbolized the grafting of each couple into God's lineage. Held in advance of our public wedding, this was an internal blessing that was officiated by Father and Mother Moon. In receiving the holy wine, we became a blessed couple.

The Marriage Blessing Ceremony of 777 couples
in Seoul, Korea on October 21, 1970.

In 1970, October 21 was a beautiful autumn day. As one of 777 couples from all over the world, we gathered in Changchung (Metropolitan) Gymnasium, a large indoor arena, for the international wedding ceremony that we called "the Blessing". With women dressed in white Korean dresses and men in dark suits, the 777 brides and grooms walked by Father and Mother, who sprinkled them with holy water. We then moved on to stand in our designated spaces. We repeated our vows in unison, promising to be faithful to God and to our spouses.

The official photo of us as a couple
participating in the Blessing Ceremony

According to our faith, we had been blessed in a marriage that made us part of God's lineage. Whatever else we did, our mission was to find others to join a new family of humankind under God, the true parent of all.

After the ceremony, we toured Seoul in commercial buses. In the evening, various international groups entertained each other in a warm exchange of music and song. In a departure from most marriage practices, certainly in the West, we waited another forty days before beginning our married life. We spent these days together in loving service to God.

Soon after the wedding, the American and European couples took a boat ride to a beautiful spot on Cheongpyeong Lake for a lakeside picnic. In 1971 this site would become the location of our church's first service hall there. Some Korean members traveled with us carrying chickens they would barbeque for us to eat. While sitting on a lovely hilltop, Father and Mother personally addressed the new couples. At that time, Father told Hugh and me that we would have good children. That prediction certainly came true!

CHAPTER 5

A Blessed Beginning:
The First Five Years

Hugh and I returned to America to assume our first of many leader-ship roles. On October 29, 1970 we were married by a magistrate in Kansas City, Missouri and obtained a marriage certificate. The legal ceremony seemed cold and impersonal after such a deeply meaningful ceremony in Korea. The blessing had given us a shared foundation for our marriage that we both trusted. We would depend on that trust as we began our life together, started to raise a family, and engaged in mission-ary work.

Opposites Attract

Hugh and I share a faith—a real tie that binds, but we are not very much alike. For us, it's true that opposites attract, and we knew we complemented each other. Hugh is a goal-oriented leader who is always focused on the mission. His character motivates him to march straight forward toward the goal. I am more inclined to take a broader view, hopefully without being distracted by details. We've joked that he moves forward without hesi-tation, and I pick up the pieces, as we climb the upward path together. Although Hugh is an activist and hands-on manager, he is also very seri-ous and contemplative. Indeed, he is an intellectual who graduated with a master's degree in public administration from Syracuse University and a Ph.D. in American history from Columbia University.

Hugh speaking at a conference

As a graduate of the School of Social Work at New York University, I'm a people person. Hugh never gets lost in the forest, but I stop to see the beauty of the trees around me. Together, we successfully conveyed the message of the Divine Principle to others and applied it to our own lives. As we shared the challenges of heavenly kingdom building, often in separate missions, we found comfort in knowing that we were there for each other. We respected each other's differences, and we needed each other's strengths. Over time, we incorporated many of each other's attributes. All I had to ask was, "What would Hugh do?" and I could adopt his decisive, uncomplicated, straightforward approach. I think he learned how to apply my inclusive decision-making process when leading a team.

On the Move

After the wedding in Korea, I returned to my job in Kansas City, and Hugh found a temporary job. We bought a house close to a campus of the

University of Missouri for a church where we taught the Divine Principle to a growing number of students. In September 1971, during our first year of marriage, our American church leaders decided that larger regional centers such as the center in Berkeley, California provided substance and strength that would promote growth. With this direction many smaller centers were consolidated into larger regional centers. Hugh and I were asked to move from Kansas City to Berkeley to help Edwin and Marie, directors of a large, fast-growing center there. With some of our Kansas City members, we joined seventy or more Berkeley members who lived in two large houses. Most of them were students at the University of California in Berkeley. Their youthful enthusiasm was appealing and contagious, attracting still more new members. During our eight months in Berkeley, we were responsible for teaching workshops to college students and other young adults.

With attendees at a workshop in Berkeley

Berkeley in the early 1970s was a hub of religious youth movements such as Children of God, Hare Krishna and Jews for Jesus—to name a few. One event during our short stint of service in California stands out. I was in charge of a monthly program to which we invited guests. Usually it was a speaker or an educational event.

One day I received a call informing me that the teenager Sat Guru Maharaji from India was coming to Berkeley and asking whether he could speak at an event in our church center. We decided to invite him. Usually we simply handed out some flyers on the University of California campus and in the surrounding area. We discovered that the Maharaji's group, later called the Divine Light Mission, was advertising extensively. That should have prepared us for the onslaught, but we never expected so large a response.

On the night of the event, young devotees began to arrive early—and they came—and came—and came, packing into the rooms of our large house. Singing and chanting, they waited for the Guru to arrive. We were used to small crowds, but this was over the top. Edwin and some church members checked the basement to be certain that the floor was holding up. We were all in a state of great anxiety, for although we were the hosts, this crowd was out of control.

It became later and later. Our anxiety was rising. Finally after what seemed like several hours the Maharaji and his entourage arrived by car. He entered the room, took his seat and began speaking. When it was all over, the people left and we all signed with relief. I was chagrined at the fiasco I had unknowingly invited! Fortunately, no one was hurt and the house was not ruined. And I was a little bit wiser.

Philadelphia

In September 1971, after a six-month period of leading workshops and supporting other programs, we were asked to take leadership of a small center in Philadelphia. We drove across the country in our trusty little Volkswagen Beetle, filled with everything we owned, where we were welcomed by George and Diane and young people with whom they were working. After two months, we found a lovely fieldstone, colonial house at 5209 Overbrook Avenue, which became the Philadelphia church center. Our family and five members lived there.

The Overbrook house where we also welcomed our first two children

Escape—Just in Time!

Our first baby was about to arrive, and we were preparing a little nursery in the Philadelphia center. On one cold windy day in January, I was at home getting everything ready for the birth, and I headed for the basement to get some supplies. I left the basement door open and cautiously descended the stairs. Suddenly, a gust of freezing wind blew the front door open. At the same time, the basement door slammed shut.

To my dismay, I was locked in! I could hear the wind howling upstairs, and I realized that the front door was standing wide open to the street. I desperately tried to push the basement door open and even tried to break the lock, but to no avail. I stacked boxes, trying to gain access to the basement casement window to crawl out, but it was too small for me with my very pregnant tummy. Feeling overwhelmed, I had no choice but to sit and wait, with the front door open and the heat running full blast. Four hours later, Hugh came home from work, alarmed to see the front door open. He called out to me and heard my reply coming from the basement. He quickly unlocked the door to find an exhausted but relieved wife.

I thank God I didn't think about the possibility of going into labor while I was in the basement, as that would have made me feel even more frantic, but it almost happened. That very night, my water broke at two o'clock a.m., and we went to the birthing center at six a.m. I gave birth to our first child, a baby girl whom we named Andrea. She was a beautiful, easy baby. Oh, how I loved the deep sense of peace and joy I felt as I cared for her. Hugh and I had taken birth classes together, and Hugh was present during the delivery. He was taking a Dale Carnegie course in public speaking and our birthing experience became a great topic for speeches.

Introducing our Founders to Philadelphia

Father Moon announced his first speaking tour in America, and Philadelphia was the second city on this tour. Our precious family time was caught up in the flurry of preparations for the visit of our Founders, the Rev. and Mrs. Moon. Rev. Moon was scheduled to speak in downtown Philadelphia in the Sheraton Hotel in just three weeks. A mobile team of fifteen members came to live in our center to prepare for the event.

During my three-day stay in the birthing center, I had already been working on public relations by calling ministers and inviting them to hear the speech. For my new baby and me, it was a hectic time with a whirlwind of activity. Then, when Andrea was four weeks old, Father and Mother arrived to stay with us in the center. They took one look at me and at Andrea, and Father said, "You need to rest. Even in Korea women rest after having a baby." Gratefully, I took his advice. Somehow, Andrea seemed to understand. God gave us a peaceful baby who slept soundly every night. During the first night after she was born, I awoke to find my new baby sleeping sweetly in the bassinet beside me. I was eagerly waiting for her to awaken for a feeding, but from the very first day, she slept until five o'clock in the morning. She awoke by grunting and stretching but seldom cried. Maybe she was happy to finally have more space!

While our Founders were in Philadelphia, they had the opportunity to meet with Pearl Buck, a well-known author. Hugh was pleased to be able to join them for this visit.

Motherhood—Making Room in My Heart

The years 1972 and 1973 were special for our family. We had a lovely center and five members living with us. Our baby, Andrea, brought much joy to everyone as we all bonded. Soon, I would have new responsibilities in my role as a mother.

Around this time, Father Moon called upon several women to travel and visit church centers. Diane and George, another couple who lived in Philadelphia, responded to this call. Diane joined a small group of women assigned to travel throughout the country to visit and support young leaders who were making valiant efforts to establish new centers. Diane's husband, George, and their eighteen-month-old son, Toby, moved into our church center.

It was a time of growth for our church and a time of growth in our home, for there were now two children, Andrea and Toby. As I breast-fed Andrea, I sometimes saw Toby watching with longing eyes, and I understood the sacrifice Diane was making to travel away from home and family on a spiritual mission. I took on my own mission—to stretch my heart and love both children with the same quality of love.

Hugh was providing leadership for our church center, while writing reports during the day as a research analyst for the Pennsylvania Economy League. I was busy caring for the two children. Life was just becoming routine when I noticed I was having trouble bending down to tie my shoes. Before Andrea was born, I had been diagnosed with a fibroid tumor, and I began to wonder if it was growing. I was feeling anxiety as I made an appointment with my gynecologist, trying to steel myself against possible bad news. After my exam, when my doctor stepped out of the exam room, I heard him tell the nurse, "Mrs. Spurgin is pregnant." To my great surprise, I was four months along!

So, do women get pregnant while breast-feeding? Although it's not common, I did, despite precautions. Now I needed to make room in my heart for one more child, and I soon began to look forward to a new life to love. Christopher was born in January, one year and one week after Andrea's birth. A cuddly little fellow, he connected with me in his own special way. I loved caring for Andrea, Toby, and Chris.

Finding personal time while caring for three children under three years of age was not easy. The book of yoga exercises for new mothers lay unopened. I looked at my post-birth tummy and wondered how I could ever find the twenty-eight minutes of uninterrupted time to focus on those exercises every day. Then I got an inspiration. Whenever the baby slept, Andrea and Toby wanted me to play with them. Why not have them play with me! If I included them in my yoga exercise program, they would experience the exercises as playtime.

With high hopes, I scheduled daily yoga exercises. All of us lined up and did each exercise together, with me calling out the instructions. The children giggled and laughed as we did the lion pose, the dog pose, and other stretching and strengthening exercises. It was a fun time for everyone and a teachable moment for me. What I had considered to be personal time for me had become a shared time of connection with the children. I deliberately used this technique as a strategy throughout my child-rearing years, and I'm still grateful for the inspiration.

Growth and Change

It was a time of growth for our family and our church. By this time, our movement in America had taken on a new name—the Unification Church. As our membership grew, the Moons planned to move their family to America.

In October 1972, the church bought the Belvedere Estate in Tarrytown, New York. To support the purchase, church members throughout America fundraised by selling candles door-to-door. Hugh and I led the fundraising effort in Philadelphia with our church members.

Our lovely family time was not to last long. On December 15, 1972, shortly before Christopher's birth, Hugh was assigned to lead a mobile evangelical team of ten members through five states in the upper Midwest region. His team was one of ten formed throughout America as part of an initiative to introduce and educate new members. Each bus team was working as part of the One World Crusade.

Hugh loved this kind of exciting mission, and he was eager to begin, even though he was sad to leave us behind. After quitting his job, he waited until after January 27, when Christopher was born, before leaving for Minneapolis to be with his team. I stayed behind in Philadelphia for the next five months, then moved with the children to join Hugh's team. Once again,

I packed our Volkswagen, this time to begin a new mission in Minnesota.

Shared Mission in the Upper Midwest

I was glad to be with Hugh and begin a three-year mission that would be one of the most successful and rewarding times of working together for our church. Hugh already had a team of ten American members, and ten more members from France, including some Americans who had joined in France, joined us to support the American providence. With our regional headquarters in Minneapolis, the team moved continuously among five states in the upper Midwest to help local centers grow.

The early seventies were years of social and political turmoil. With dedication and enthusiasm, our team of young adults witnessed to many youth who were seeking God and purpose in their lives. The sincerity of the new recruits was beautiful. As they joined us, we rejoiced and worked even harder to expand God's kingdom on earth. These Midwestern youth were solid, responsible, stable Christians who responded to our message with earnest enthusiasm. We sang, prayed, studied, witnessed, taught the Divine Principle, played sports, fundraised, and laughed a lot.

Another Speaking Tour

Hugh and his OWC team worked tirelessly to organize preparations and promotional activities for Father Moon's new twenty-one-city tour in the fall of 1973, and their hard work was blessed with success. On three nights, November 30, December 1 and December 2, Father Moon spoke to overflow crowds at a very large auditorium on the campus of the University of Minnesota. In the preface to *Christianity in Crisis: New Hope,* Dr. Bo Hi Pak, a Special Assistant to Father Moon, wrote regarding those three speeches:

Rev. Sun Myung Moon's 21-city speaking tour of America has been a dazzling success….. His message truly kindled a fire in the hearts of thousands of young people across the country. We saw hundreds of college students jam-packed into West Bank Auditorium at the University of Minnesota, listening fervently to every word spoken. Deep seriousness shadowed their faces. For the inspiring message of Rev. Moon not only attracts a young audience, but it then holds them spellbound and draws them inexorably back for the second and third nights.

Prior to those speeches, the Moons hosted a banquet for many VIPs. After the third talk, a victory celebration was held at a McDonald's Restaurant.

*The victory Celebration at McDonald's
with Rev. and Mrs. Moon.*

During our founder's visit to Minneapolis, on November 30 the church published on November 30 a statement by Father Moon in full-page ads in twenty-one cities, with the headline "America in Crisis: Answer to Watergate." In the prayer room in our center, Dr. Bo Hi Pak, interpreter and assistant to Father Moon, read the statement to a few members. Hugh was there, but at that time I was traveling as an Itinerary Worker in the Northwest states. In December, Hugh went to Washington to participate in a fast and candlelight vigil calling on the American people to forgive, love and unite with one another.

Heart of a Region

The church was growing in our region. In December 1973, we rented a place in Spirit Lake, Iowa, where members from each of the five states could bring guests for weekend workshops. Potential new members who wanted to continue studying stayed for a follow-up, seven-day workshop. At Spirit Lake, we also set up a small nursery where our children stayed with a caregiver, while Hugh and I traveled with the team. I often did advance and follow-up work in the states. Each weekend, with great anticipation and joy in our hearts, we were together again. Hugh still gave Divine Principle lectures, and I counseled members from our region, but we spent every minute we could with our children.

During our three years of work in the Upper Midwest, we felt God's joy and spirit flowing, and many new members joined the church. More than 300 young people from our region went out to various missions throughout the country and world.

A Potato Fast

I often visited the state centers in our region where idealistic young leaders were trying out their wings. When I arrived at one small center in South

Dakota, I was greeted with a "potato fast providence." The young members there had decided that eating from a 100-pound bag of potatoes for a week made for cheap living. "Potatoes do have a lot of nutrients," one of them said, defending the plan.

I joined them on their potato fast until I realized they were spending all their time finding potato recipes and cooking. We had potato cakes, fried potatoes, French fries, mashed potatoes, au gratin potatoes, and on and on. "You are saving money, but you are wasting all your time being creative in the kitchen," I said. With that, the potato fast ended.

As part of an eight-city Day of Hope tour, Rev. Moon was scheduled to speak on September 18, 1974 at a large rally in Madison Square Garden. In order to prepare for the event, Hugh took seventy members of his International One World Crusade team in six 15-seat vans to New York City to campaign for the event. On the streets of Harlem, they canvassed and distributed tickets for the event. They stayed in a hotel located near Columbia University.

An Amazing Purchase!

While Hugh was in New York City preparing for the Madison Square Garden speech, I stayed home to look for a workshop facility we could purchase for our region. For just $11,000, I found a three-story brick school building that had been vacant for two years for sale in Greenville, Iowa. We were especially happy that it had a new addition with a nice cafeteria, kitchen, and several classrooms. Excitedly, I called Hugh with the news of my find. He agreed that we should buy it. Following a successful MSG rally of 20,000 people, we turned that school building into a wonderful weekend workshop facility that accommodated several hundred people. It became the spiritual birthplace for many new members. The school provided a lovey and adequate space for many enjoyable meetings and activities. The main floor had a large lecture room, cafeteria and kitchen. We converted the second and third floor classrooms for use as separate sleeping quarters for men and women. On the third floor, we also created a nursery for children from the region, including our own. They stayed with Mary and Lynn who were capable and dedicated caregivers. We hung cheerful juvenile wallpaper on the walls and furnished a room to serve as our own weekend home.

*Members assembled in front of the building in
Greenville, Iowa on 1 January 1974*

Many members have fond memories of their experiences in Greenville, Iowa. It was like a vacation home where they could meet with friends from throughout the region, share stories, and have fun, as well as conduct educational programs. Even the children remember it as a special place. After we moved to Barrytown, New York, five-year-old Chris could be heard trying to convince his camp friends that Greenville, Iowa was the place to live!

Participants in a weekend workshop program

Bad News with a Silver Lining

After holding workshops in Greenville for two years, our purchase money was still in escrow because the state government continued to research the previous sale of the property. The title search uncovered a problem, not with the sale to us, but with the sale to the seller from whom we had bought the school. As a result, we were unable to retain ownership.

At first, we were dismayed, but our inability to buy the school turned out to be a blessing. The facility had served our purpose beautifully, but the providence had changed. The IOWC teams were being called to serve on a national level, under a new structure, and we no longer needed the property. Our escrow money was returned. We had made good use of it for a long time without having to pay for it. We had maintained and improved the property, and we thought of these renovations as an offering. Everyone was happy. God works in mysterious ways!

The years between 1970 and 1975 had been full of growth on a personal, family and church level. We had started our married life in a small center in Kansas City, followed by successive missions in Berkeley, Philadelphia, and in the Upper Midwest centered on Minneapolis. In the midst of all of that we had participated in Father Moon's speech at Madison Square Garden. Our lives had been enriched by facing challenges and successes together, and we had been blessed by becoming parents of two beautiful children. Soon we would be called to assignments that would test our hearts in a new way.

CHAPTER 6

A Challenging Mission

In 1974, the church bought a large facility on beautiful grounds in Barrytown, New York, where members participated in a 120-day training program. Reverend Ken Sudo, an elder in the Japanese church, served as the director and lecturer for the training program. Graduates of the program were sent to cities throughout America as pioneer missionaries to initiate or support new church centers. In May 1975, I accepted a call to take part in one of the large training programs. In attendance were many young members. I was part of a smaller group of long-term members who were preparing for exceptionally challenging missions as Itinerary Workers, which involved leaving my family and traveling to various cities in order to mentor young pioneer missionaries in America. A nursery was established in the gatehouse on the Barrytown campus, and we moved our children and their caregiver, Mary, there.

Forty-Days in the Wilderness

Our training with everyone included Divine Principle lectures, practice teaching, prayer vigils, and evenings of fellowship. Our small group spent several days selling flowers to practice fundraising. As the final part of our training, each member of our group was assigned to work alone in a New England city to do pioneer missionary work for forty days.

I was dropped off in Waterbury, Connecticut, with a little "seed money" to last for the first few days and a written daily schedule designed to keep me focused on my work as a missionary. On the first lonely night in my pioneer city, I went to bed in my hotel room thinking about what the next day would bring. I would rise early, find a room for the next forty days, fundraise enough to pay for it, and move with my teaching easel and suitcase before noon when I had to leave the hotel. It was a restless night. I arose early to find a newspaper to begin my search for a room.

Fortunately, I found a third-floor room, and my new landlord kindly gave me a ride to pick up my suitcase and easel. Thus began my forty-day pioneer experience of street speaking, witnessing, teaching, and fundraising to support myself. On weekends, I gathered with other pioneers and guests at a regional workshop center where Divine Principle lectures were given.

One of the hardest parts about the pioneer training was being separated from Hugh and the children. Hugh and I had worked apart before, but never for that long a time without seeing each other, and I had always been with the children, at least every weekend. After the forty days passed, I was elated to see my family again!

We Were Mothers and Mentors

During the 1970s, our Unification movement touched the hearts of many idealistic youth who were searching for meaning in life. In the Divine Principle teaching, they had found it! After they studied and gained experience, usually at an established church center, they were sent out across America to start new centers where still more young people could find God's love and a purpose for their lives.

To provide cohesion, continuity, and encouragement for these young leaders, Father Moon asked some of the women from the early marriage blessings to serve as Itinerary Workers, or IWs, in designated regions. I was one of those who responded to this call. After completing our program at Barrytown, we were to begin the mission for which we had been preparing. There was no fixed time as to when that mission would end.

With mixed emotions and heavy hearts, we placed our precious young children in a nursery that was set up for their care in the gatehouse on the Barrytown property. On September 20, 1975, I left to serve as an Itinerary Worker to mentor and support new leaders in various cities in a region centered on Denver, Colorado as the headquarters.

Traveling and visiting centers in several states as an IW gave me an opportunity to bond with many young members and leaders as we worked and problem-solved together. My professional training as a social worker was a great blessing. On a deeper level, my walk with God gave me a source of wisdom and guidance that I knew came from beyond myself.

Understanding the Meaning of Sacrifice

There was an internal reason for our assignments as IWs. Father Moon had a purposeful style of living, and he taught that by making personal sacrifices in service to God's providence, we could bring many blessings to the work. By asking us to undertake this mission as a sacrificial offering, we were connecting with a higher providence and following the example of our Founders. By doing this, we would inherit greater spiritual power in our lives and work.

Awareness of the internal, spiritual reality connected to every aspect of our external lives is not second nature to American people. Therefore, we had to make this offering in faith. It helped to remember the sacrifices made by our men and women in the military service, and by their families, for the sake of our nation. We were in a spiritual war to save America from spiritual downfall.

Life as an Itinerary Worker

Constant traveling among cities and states for months at a time as an itinerary worker was physically exhausting. At each stop, adjusting my approach to meet people where they were required flexibility and creativity. Some of the young people I worked with had the essential comforts of home in their small centers, but some were existing on the barest minimum. Some were confident and eager, while others were less sure of themselves. In all cases, there was a sincere desire to do their best for God and for those they had come to reach.

I faced the greatest challenge in my own heart. I admired the sacrificial faith of our missionaries and was lifted up by the enthusiasm and joy of their students as they awakened to faith. I had no doubt that what I was doing had value. But deep within, there was a persistent ache that I could share with few. It was the constant longing to be with my children.

Fatal Accident

In my first assignment, I had to call on all my strength. In October 1975, I was traveling within the southwest region where the center in Denver, Colorado served as the headquarters. Arriving on a Sunday, I walked into the church office to see the church leader sitting by the phone with his head in his hands. With a grief-stricken expression on his face, he told me that he had just received the news that a group of members and their guests had been in a vehicle accident while returning to the center from a workshop. People had lost their lives.

The next morning, the headline in a New Mexico newspaper read, "Six Killed on Route 66, Six Miles East of Tucumcari." In addition to four people in one car, a couple in the oncoming car were killed. In a state of shock, I immediately flew to New Mexico to bring solace to the devastated members and offer any help I could. I participated in notifying parents, preparing for funerals, dealing with the media and official notices, and reaching out to everyone who was involved. Whenever I recall those days in New Mexico, I still feel the weight of this tragedy.

The Blue-Sky Hotel

During the workshop program at Barrytown, the Reverend Sudo had talked about learning to adapt to your situation. He joked about sleeping under the stars as living in the "Blue Sky Hotel." As I traveled among the states to visit the young pioneers, I came across someone doing just that. Picking me up at the bus station, Tom announced that I could not stay with him in the place where he lived, but he had some friends with whom I could spend the night. I ended up as the surprise guest of three girls who shared an attic apartment.

I learned that Tom had made his home under a tree some distance behind a supermarket. He had built a shelter from cardboard boxes taken from a dumpster at the market, and his clothes hung in a bag from a tree limb. His money and the items he sold to raise money to live on were in a container in a covered box buried in a hole he had dug. He spent his days meeting people and teaching them the Divine Principle in coffee shops. During the night—you guessed it—he camped out in his blue-sky hotel.

I reported to Rev. Sudo that I thought the blue-sky camping out had taken precedence over the mission. I hated to rain on Tom's parade, since his creativity was impressive, but I had to deliver Rev. Sudo's message that the blue-sky hotel condition should end as soon as possible.

On the Mountaintop

Occasionally, a leader from national headquarters would visit a regional headquarters to give inspirational talks and encouragement to the region's pioneers. On one such occasion, we were called together as a region for an all-night prayer vigil, in the wintertime, on a mountain in Oklahoma.

As the Itinerary Worker in the region, I attended the vigil. All night prayer conditions always require focus and creativity to make the time with our Heavenly Father meaningful. It was so cold that it was easy to be distracted by trying to keep warm. I prayed, sang, and shifted my feet back and forth, but the night became longer and longer. It was hard not to watch the clock. I thought, "I must get some spiritual fire going to keep my mind off the cold and make this condition meaningful!"

As I prayed, I thought about the ancestors of the people who suffered as the West was settled, and I decided to be a channel for the liberation of the resentment they might hold. While praying, I pictured them in my mind's eye walking past the throne of God with heads bowed. I made up a simple little song that I sang throughout the rest of the night. As I visualized each person walking by, I sang, "Let them be pure and free before thee, Lord. Let them be pure and free before thee." The night passed much faster.

Trying Times for our Young Church

The 1970s was a decade of unrest in general. The war in Vietnam had stirred up anti-war sentiment, and youth were searching for a purpose in life. Building a heavenly kingdom of peace on earth was appealing to such seekers, and God stirred their hearts. Amid such cultural turmoil, the Unification Church centers offered inspiration and refuge.

The pioneer activities that brought many young people to hear the Divine Principle teachings caught the attention of the American public, and some parents of young members strongly disapproved, fearing the changes occurring in their sons' and daughters' lives. In 1976, the Unification Church started receiving negative attention from all sides.

Opponents falsely accused Rev. and Mrs. Moon of using mind-control on new recruits. There were some who paid vigilante-style deprogrammers to physically kidnap, confine, and forcibly pressure their children to renounce their faith. In opposition to new religions, the Cult Awareness Network was established to coordinate persecution of the Unification Church and other new religious groups. They justified violent, abusive actions against members by saying that the Unification church was a cult where young people were brainwashed into becoming members. Eventually, the church won several major court cases. Hugh wrote an article on the misuse of terms such as brainwashing and mind-control to describe the legitimate conversion experience that new Unification members had experienced.

Conference Connections

Between October 1975 and November 1976, church leaders went to Tarrytown, New York each month for a leadership conference with Father Moon. During this time, my husband was a graduate student at Unification Theological Seminary, or UTS, and he lived in the seminary dormitory in Barrytown. It was a comfort to me that the nursery was in the gatehouse on the UTS campus, which allowed Hugh to spend time with our children.

For all the mothers working as Itinerary Workers, the monthly conferences provided brief but precious time we could spend with our husbands and children. For me, each conference was like an oasis in the desert where I could connect with our Founders, other leaders, my IW colleagues, and Hugh, but most of all, with my children.

At one conference, Father Moon said that the Itinerary Workers should report to him on a regular basis. Contemplating this, I decided to make a report form and send the completed report to him and headquarters at the end of each weekly visit. I did this for the rest of my IW career, even though I never received feedback. Years later Colonel Han, an assistant and translator for Father Moon, said to me, "Nora, I miss your reports. I used to read them to Father every week." I was humbled to hear this. Looking back, I think my reports created a connection with Father Moon that made future communications easier.

The Lighter Side of our Founder

Although deeply serious about his mission, Father Moon also had a unique sense of humor. Sometimes during a leaders' conference, he would say something funny to get everyone's attention. I was the frequent object of his wake-up calls to his audience. He made one of his funniest comments when he was encouraging the state leaders to promote the fishing business that he had established. As he was encouraging them to sell tuna, he caught my eye in the audience and said, "Nora, will you sell tuna on the street corner?" Then, with a grin, he added, "In the snow?" He had caught the attention of the audience as he went on, "In a bikini?" I still hear about that joke!

An Example

At one Belvedere conference, during a long sermon by Father Moon, I needed to use the restroom. Looking around for the least obvious exit path, I glanced up and caught Father Moon's eye. He seized the moment! I knew he would call me out.

"Nora, what did I just say?" Of course, I did not know. I tried frantically to catch my last memory, but I was unsuccessful. "Father, I don't know." He then pointed out that some people were sleeping during his sermon.

These personal exchanges with Father Moon made me feel close to him, as a daughter would feel toward a father.

A Welcome Addition

I traveled and visited members on my itinerary circuit until six weeks before the birth of our next child. I then went to Barrytown where Hugh, five-year-old Andrea and four-year-old Chris were living. On December

16, 1976, I gave birth to our second daughter—third child. At our request, Father Moon suggested that we name her Ameri, representing America. She always loved her name. She had beautiful eyes, and she was a chubby little one whom we called "her royal roundness."

The dolls in our family! Andrea with her new sister, Ameri

After six weeks with my family, I packed up my sweet little bundle of comfort and joy and took her with me to the mission field. This time around, I was working in New England, and I was able to drive, so I kept Ameri with me until she was four months old. This was a precious time with my newborn baby, but all good things must end.

After four months on the road, Ameri's needs became greater, and I decided it was better for her and for me to take her back to the nursery. She had been such a comfort to me, sleeping with me every night, but she now needed more space and equipment. Unlike Andrea, who slept all night, Ameri woke up every two hours to breastfeed. Maybe she was sleeping too close to the bottle! With tears, I took my precious baby to join Andrea and Chris in the nursery at Barrytown, where Rosemary, a maternal German girl, cared for her for the next six months of her life.

We continued our itinerary work for six more months, when in January we were told that our service condition was over. There are no words to describe the relief I felt at being with the children again.

CHAPTER 7

A House Becomes a Home

Being away from the children had been the hardest experience of my life. Yes, it was an adjustment to be instantly in charge of two young children and a baby. Yes, we would be living in unusual circumstances, but we were together. That is what mattered.

One House, Two Families

The beautiful grounds and surroundings of the Barrytown campus of the seminary had served as a home base while our children were cared for there in the gatehouse nursery. With the end of the IW mission, there was no further need for a nursery, but neither the Jones nor the Spurgin family had a home, so it made sense for the gatehouse to become a duplex for both families.

Betsy Jones, my good friend and fellow traveler, had shared the same course as an IW, and our children had been in the church nursery together. She and I had joined our church the same year. Betsy's husband, Farley, and my husband had been students at the seminary. Hugh graduated with the first class on July 1, 1977, and Farley graduated the following year. Both couples had participated in the 777 Couples Blessing Ceremony. There are too many connections to name. In many ways, it felt like the Spurgins and the Jones were one family.

*The Barrytown campus of UTS was our home for many years,
while Hugh worked on his doctorate at Columbia University.*

*The gatehouse on the UTS campus served as the nursery for our children
and later as the home we shared with the Jones family.*

When we moved into the gatehouse, our combined six children, who already knew the gatehouse as home, were waiting to greet us. Betsy's husband, Farley, was on a mission in England, and Hugh was in New York City working on a PhD in American history at Columbia University, so Betsy and I were the two heads of the new household.

The children were used to living like one big family, so that's how they treated us, each other, and the house. Betsy and I had a need to create separate Jones and Spurgin identities as we carved out spaces in a house with one kitchen, one bathroom, and four bedrooms. We made sensitive efforts to reestablish our nuclear families, strengthening the parent-child bonds, while sharing the main living spaces.

We made a schedule where one of us cooked a meal for everyone and ate dinner with her own children while the other mother supervised her children's baths and prepared for bedtime. After bath time and pajamas, the other family had their dinner together and did both sets of dishes. This pattern was reversed the next day. Our system worked, and we plowed through the challenges of living together!

To have some individual family quality time, we sometimes took our own children out for short day trips or took them upstairs where each family had two rooms. At other times, we all gathered in the living room to share the joy of watching our two families interact in great creative fun. Once they came downstairs in grass skirts made of toilet paper to entertain us with a dance.

Mischief could become catastrophe with the combined efforts of little hands and minds. This was the case when the kids joined forces to hook up an open gallon of paint to a rope attached to a door handle. Of course, when we opened the door, the paint spilled all over our newly carpeted floor! We finally restored the carpet, but both Betsy and I were pregnant at the time, so cleaning up was daunting. Such pranks were instrumental in bringing our children together in a friendship that continues today.

Our communal living was more difficult for Betsy than for me, for I was one of nine children, and she was one of two. Once Betsy's mother visited and immediately got busy cleaning what she called, "Betsy's stove." I felt a little embarrassed that a stranger was cleaning *my* stove! Looking back at this, however, I realize I should have just been appreciative of her serving both of us through her love for her daughter.

Later, the Jones family moved to an apartment in one of several houses the church had purchased in Tarrytown, New York, called Gracemere Hall, and our family stayed in Barrytown. Edwin and Marie Ang and their family also lived in a house on the UTS grounds, and there were other families there. We quickly found ourselves working together to entertain everyone's children.

Camp Sunrise!

In the summer of 1977, Marie and I met with several other mothers to make a daily plan for our children. At one such meeting, one of the children suggested naming our summer program *Camp Sunrise*. Each family then decided to invite a friend to stay with them and spend two weeks at our summer camp at Barrytown with the children who already lived there. All the children had great fun, and the mothers also enjoyed the experience.

The following summer, Linna Rapkins and Betsy Jones joined us for two weeks with their families. With the inspiration of the mothers who lived on the Barrytown campus, Camp Sunrise made its debut and grew to be a camp of two hundred children. With the utilization of seminary facilities, it was a beautiful, refreshing and nourishing setting for the children to enjoy one another. Year after year, new families came. To make it work, we used the UTS facilities, including dormitories, lecture rooms, dining hall, kitchen, swimming pool, and even the stables for horseback riding. Many mothers joined our staff and several young people served as camp counselors.

In an era when the church was facing strong opposition, we tried to protect our children, but they could feel the negative attitudes of some of their classmates and even some of their teachers, at school. The opportunity to be at Camp Sunrise with others who shared their faith was liberating.

The children of Camp Sunrise have so many precious memories of their experiences during those two weeks each summer. They made life-long friends, and many look back on their time there as holding some of their fondest memories of childhood. They played sports, took trips, created dramatic performances, and attended classes on religious values and principles. As mothers, we valued the opportunity to give our full attention to our children and their education and entertainment.

Campers at Barrytown

Lisa and Susan, members of the camp staff, wrote a beautiful song that became our camp anthem. The song still rings in my ears and brings a smile to my face. In my mind's eye, I can still see the children singing it with enthusiasm as they rode together in a hay wagon.

Here are the words to the song:

Sunrise Song

I climb the hill and seek the sun's first rays
I'm filled with joy that camp begins today
We come from all around, from distant shores
We'll share our laughter, love, and more
For we are sunrise (sunrise) sons and daughters
Sunrise (sunrise) children of the sun
We'll swim and hike and play the whole day through
We laugh and sing and pray, our hearts are true
And as we watch the fire late at night
We'll feel our love is glowing bright
For we are sunrise (sunrise) sons and daughters
Sunrise (sunrise) children of the sun
When I go home, I'll climb that same old hill
I'll watch that sun and feel you with me still
And as you're watching too so far away
You'll know our love will always stay

Lasting Value

Linna and Marie, both former teachers, Betsy a nurse, and I played major roles in the development of Camp Sunrise. After we outgrew the facilities in Barrytown, we moved the camp to a church site in Harriman State Park, also in New York. By this time, we had new leadership, including older children of church members.

Though we had worked on missions much of the time, sometimes separated from our families, we always longed to be with them. Juggling the roles of spouse, mother, and missionary was never easy, and it had sometimes brought conflict and heartache.

Camp Sunrise had given us an opportunity to have it both ways. We were undertaking an important mission by providing a safe, stimulating, and spiritually oriented place for many children, and also be close to our own children and watch them grow and flourish among others who shared their values.

This precious time of living at Barrytown and working with other church mothers, and sometimes fathers, to support our children gave all our families a stronger foundation. In future years, I would again travel and work full time for the church, but in Camp Sunrise, mission and family needs met. This experience helped me to understand that, on a deep level, serving the world meant serving my family, and serving my family meant serving the world.

CHAPTER 8

International Missionaries

Wedding Vows

1. We pledge that we will become an eternal husband and wife, consummating the ideal of God's creation with absolute fidelity.

2. We pledge that we will inherit and maintain the tradition of family unity and pass this tradition on to the future generations of our family and all humankind.

3. We pledge that as true parents we will raise our children to live up to God's will and educate them to be sexually abstinent until marriage.

4. We pledge that we will support all families to uplift these ideals, beyond race, religion, and nation, by participating in the blessing of marriage, helping create the Kingdom of God on earth and in heaven.

Missionaries Promoting World Peace

In February 1975, eighteen hundred couples from all over the world gathered in Seoul, Korea and pledged to establish God-centered families in fidelity to each other and in service to the world. Most of the couples from America had served as church leaders in some capacity. They were intelligent young men and women who had honed their leadership skills through training and working in pioneer centers throughout the country. They had worked as leaders in their states, as staff at headquarters, or leaders of church organizations. Father Moon, true to his purposeful lifestyle, would again sacrifice American leadership for the sake of a larger cause—the world.

Providential Assignments, Authentic Results

After the blessing of the eighteen hundred couples, these newly married, idealistic, well-educated, and talented young leaders were sent out to every nation in the world. Not only were they committed to bringing the Divine Principle to their assigned countries, they had an internal mission.

The German and Japanese movements also sent a member to each country. Three strangers, one American, one German, and one Japanese person, shared a worldview and embraced the teachings of Father and Mother Moon, but they did not share either language or culture. They were asked to work together to make a condition of harmony and unity as a foundation for world peace. What a mission! The missionaries traveled to their countries in the face of many challenges. Some established thriving church centers while others floundered. Some faced persecution and even imprisonment. Many lived on meager provisions.

After they had worked in their countries for three years, the newly established daily newspaper, *The Newsworld*, sent representatives to train them to become foreign correspondents. This provided the missionaries with a position that allowed them to meet leaders in their countries, and it provided The News World, which later became the *New York City Tribune*, with on-the-spot reports from everywhere in the world. As usual, Father Moon's directives were multifaceted and brilliant.

International Team Visiting Missionaries

Our Founders understood the sacrificial lives of these missionaries and knew they needed a heart connection to the larger church. Many were in isolated and challenging circumstances, and they needed encouragement, support, wise counsel, a compassionate listening ear, and sometimes the comfort of a motherly touch. To my surprise, I received a call on February 10, 1978, inviting me to become a member of a three-person team that would for forty days visit missionaries in Oceania and Southeast Asia.

Team members were Larry Moffit, Mr. Watanabe, and myself. Our first stop was Japan, then on to Australia, Thailand, India, Iran, and Hong Kong. In each country, we met with the American, German, and Japanese missionaries of the various surrounding countries.

It was a wonderful team to travel with, and we worked well together. When things got too intense, Larry's sense of humor lightened the atmosphere wherever we went. Mr. Watanabe was easy to talk to and a welcome presence for the worldwide missionaries from Japan. I could lend my experience and bring a mother's heart.

This assignment would be one of the most emotionally intense six weeks of my life. Upon my return, it would take me an equal amount of time to digest and absorb my experiences.

An Anxious Flight

After spending several days together at the Japanese missionary department, Larry, Mr. Watanabe, and I began our itinerary by heading for Australia. On this trip, there was a disconnect that brought me some anxiety. We were going to arrive at Narita International Airport in Japan from separate locations. I checked in but did not see my traveling companions. Nearing the top of the escalator, I sighed with relief when I saw them approaching the bottom of the escalator. Knowing they were not far behind me, I moved on to check in and board the plane.

After settling into the flight, I searched the plane without finding my companions, and the flight attendant said they were not on the plane's list of passengers. The plane was overbooked, and I found myself alone on my way to an unfamiliar part of the world. With dismay, I realized that Larry was carrying the flight itinerary, and all I had with me was a ticket to change planes in Hong Kong. There would be a two-hour layover in Singapore in the middle of the night. I had seldom felt as alone as I did during the entire seventeen-hour trip.

When I finally landed in Melbourne, I was relieved when church members met me at the airport and said Larry and Mr. Watanabe would arrive the next day. In the end, I spent the first day of my mission having a wonderful time with the Australian family and international missionaries from surrounding countries in Oceania. Once united, our team shared an uplifting visit with the missionaries who gathered on our first stop.

Kolkata, India

From the very beginning, our visit to Kolkata (Calcutta), India was filled with challenges. Our taxi ride from the airport ended with a big fight between our missionary and the driver. The driver wanted to overcharge us to the extent that he returned in the evening to collect more money. I learned that this was a common occurrence for them, but it was an uncomfortable confrontation for the team.

After we settled in, Sara, the American missionary, invited me to go with her to the post office. On the way, we walked through a crowd of angry protesting workers. Sara advised me, "Hold your purse tight, as they use razors to slit the bottom of your purse." Wow! How on guard we had to be! We stood in a long line at the post office to avoid the stamps being ripped off the letter from the outdoor box.

On our return to the center, a little boy walked beside me, rubbing the stub of his amputated arm against my arm and begging for money. Sara said, "Don't give him money, or he and other beggars will follow you everywhere you go." I looked into his sad eyes and thought of my own children. It was hard not to give him money. He followed us for several blocks until we lost him by hiding in a small shop.

Kolkata was definitely a place of poverty. Women cooked in the streets over cow dung patties, which created a pungent haze every evening. After five days, I caught the flu and felt so sick that I just wanted to lie under the table at our final dinner. I was sorry to be so miserable and kept thinking, "I am here to bring them encouragement, and I can hardly stand up."

I felt guilty because I was eager to leave, but I will forever be in awe of Sara's spirit and the spirit of the other missionaries in India. Sara became a professor at a university in Texas when she returned to America, and we are still in touch.

Iran

We went on to Teheran, where Susan (the American missionary) found antibiotics for me and nursed me back to health. During the first couple of days of our visit, I felt embarrassed to be so needy, but with Susan's care, I was healing. In this country, twelve wonderful young men and one of their sisters lived together in a church center. They were learning, teaching, and doing missionary work. Even though we were in an Islamic environment that denied missionary activity, there was interest and enthusiasm.

Meeting with enthusiastic members in Iran

Thailand and Hong Kong

In Bangkok, Thailand, we found another thriving center. Jack and Eva had established a strenuous standard of devotion and spiritual activity. In this center, I met an impressive young follower, a young Thai doctor who was to become the leader of the church in Thailand. In later years, he would be imprisoned for his faith. Missionaries from the surrounding nations gathered to share their stories and learn to become foreign correspondents for The *Newsworld* (later named the *New York Tribune*). George, a missionary who joined us from Singapore, shared news of his work in a growing center there.

Hong Kong, our last stop, was a lesson in Chinese culture, and our visit to the center provided an experience more akin to our experience in America.

Dedication and Sacrifice

The moving missionary stories that our members shared touched me deeply. We also shared our stories with them. We laughed, we cried, and we learned about each other's cultures, including economies and religious practices. We tried different foods. We appreciated each other's successes and felt each other's sorrows. We learned about their hopes and plans, and we heard about their disappointments when they felt unsupported or forgotten.

We listened with compassion to their stories about challenging health issues and sufferings from persecution. We were in awe of their passion and sacrifice in bringing the Divine Principle teaching and vision to each of the nations they had come to love and serve.

I began to see patterns in the stories I heard. The Japanese, German, and American missionaries each had different perspectives based on their experience and cultural background. It was sometimes hard for them to accept each other's viewpoints, and it took much growth in my heart to see the reason God put them together.

The American missionary felt unsupported when the Japanese missionary spent so much time at home focusing on the internal foundation for the country by praying, reading, and studying. The Japanese missionary felt that the American's focus on going out, meeting people, teaching, and speaking in order to make the external foundation was lacking in the deeper spiritual aspect of the mission. The German missionary, often younger in age and church membership, was caught in the middle, wondering whom to support.

Only with increasing experience and maturity could they see the value of each person's approach. God had placed them together in missions that required them to expand their hearts and minds.

These brave young people shared stories of incredible and miraculous experiences. Most of the German missionaries were young girls, and some were just out of high school. While working alone in lands foreign to them, it was sometimes difficult to protect their virginity or even their lives. There were stories of unlikely connections leading to daring rescues. One young girl was caught between borders of two countries, unable to get into either of them. Fortunately, a pilot flying a small plane landed near her and offered to take her to her destination. Through these experiences, they had felt the presence of God in ways that people seldom do. Most of us do not have as urgent a need for God's intervention that these missionaries had.

My life was deeply touched and enriched by our visits with the international missionaries, and I am forever grateful to have been a small part of their heroic endeavor to bring the Divine Principle to everyone in the world.

This was one of the profound experiences that helped me to grow in compassion and broaden my thinking about the church and its real potential to change the world. I had seen firsthand what heart and faith could achieve under the most stressful and challenging circumstances. This was to be an important part of my perspective as a spouse, mother, and church worker for the rest of my life.

CHAPTER 9

Family Matters

The family unit is at the center of the Divine Principle teaching, and during the next decade, family would be my focus, whether I was giving birth, counseling others about marriage and family concerns, setting up a new department to support church families, or leading a bus team of women missionaries who were trying to balance family and mission priorities.

There would be a stretch of time when I had my own home, a stable job in the church, and a pleasant commute. My children would grow and begin to branch out. There would be close calls in our family and profound tragedies in families we loved. Through all that happened, I would continue to learn.

A New Joy

After such a heart-stretching trip to visit the international missionaries, it was a great comfort to return to my little home in the gatehouse. I continued to raise our children and serve as a counselor, when needed, at the seminary.

With great happiness, I began preparing for the fourth little one in our growing family. On April 12, 1979, a wonderful little boy joined us. Born three weeks early, he weighed five pounds, fifteen ounces, and he had no hair, making him look a little "unfinished." The kids called him our "alien baby," but he lost that name when his hair grew in.

Hugh was named after his father, and I asked him whether he would like to name our little son "Hugh Dwayne Spurgin, III." He would not consider it. We asked Father Moon to provide a name, and the message came back, "His name should be High." It seemed to us to be a version of Hugh!

We scoured the name book for a second name to go with it, eventually deciding on "Linn," so he could be "High-Linn," if he chose, but he always called himself "High." He had a soft, mellow personality, and some of the students from the seminary came to the house to hold him when they wanted to recover from stress. One such student, Linda, wrote a poem about him called, "Little Snowflake"!

*Our family dressed in Caribbean outfits that we bought
while attending a conference in Jamaica.*

International Matching—Preparing the Candidates

Excitement was in the air in the spring of 1979, when we learned there would be a large matching ceremony on May 13. Even though High was barely a month old, I wouldn't have time for my own family for a while, as I was among several women called to national headquarters to help prepare for this much-anticipated event. My psychiatric social work training and therapy experience were put to good use as we processed data, reviewed applications, established eligibility, prepared educational materials, and counseled some of the matching candidates.

The primary mission of our Founders was to establish the marriage blessing on earth to bring all humanity into God's lineage, and they consistently worked toward this goal. Hundreds of members from throughout America would be taking part in the next blessing, and there would be more matchings on December 29, 1980, June 29, 1982, and March 27, 1987. In February 1988, there would be yet another matching, this time in Korea.

The Process

On the day of the 1979 matching, candidates from throughout America gathered in the New Yorker, a well-known hotel now owned by the church. Renovations made the ballroom a beautiful space for such a significant event. A group of newly arrived young women from Japan joined the group, in addition to members from all over the world. They all found places in the grand ballroom. When Father Moon entered the room, he was greeted with thousands of eager faces and an atmosphere of great anticipation.

Candidates were seated on the floor, with men on Father Moon's left and women on the right. Each candidate was trusting God to choose an eternal partner for them through Father Moon. One young woman told me, "When I looked up, I saw golden threads leading from one person to another, and I watched Father Moon's eyes following those threads as he chose couples."

A young man said he was sitting behind a column, out of Father's line of vision, when Father asked a young woman to stand up. He searched the men's side of the room, looking for a match, and he seemed to be looking for someone in particular. The young man moved into view and was at once chosen as the match for this young woman.

Many participants told stories of spiritual connections as they were matched. After each selection, the potential couple was guided to a get-acquainted area in the balcony of the ballroom where they could talk before accepting or rejecting the match. Most accepted.

Sometimes Father Moon interacted with the candidates, asking questions such as, "Would you like a Japanese wife?" or, "He is shorter than you are. Is that okay?" or, "This person has a disability. Will you love him?" It was moving to watch all the personal interactions.

Throughout the day and night, Rev. Moon called candidates to the center of the room. Each person held a color-coded card with a number and identifying information. When a match was suggested, the couple came forward, made a slight bow of recognition, and moved to the front of the room where they turned in their cards. I was on the team sitting at the table to receive the cards, staple them together, and file them. As matched couples came toward me, I saw smiling faces, though some expressions were serious, thoughtful, or even anxious.

The following day, couples were everywhere, sitting in the hotel lobby, walking on the streets of New York City, and having lunch across the street at McDonalds or in other nearby restaurants. God must have been happily watching his children.

A New Department

After the matchings and blessing of 2,075 couples on July 1, 1982, at Madison Square Garden, the church established a new office as a central point of contact and support for the young couples. There was a need to identify and address challenges they would face in working out their relationships. Many church couples were from different nations, cultures, and races. My new assignment was to create a Blessed Family Department at the church headquarters.

Betsy Jones, who was a psychiatric nurse, joined the department as well. Both of us used our education, professional training, and good intentions to guide and counsel the new couples on their marital journey. We were available to them through the office, and we received many counseling calls at home. Most of the couples who contacted us had a strong sense of commitment to their marriages, and they were willing to work out problems that arose.

The Blessed Family Department further supported couples and families by publishing the *Blessing Quarterly* to provide education and communication. Later we published the *Blessed Family Journal.* For both publications we collected and wrote articles about marriage and family life and solicited articles and announcements from couples and families in the church.

We counseled couples, spoke to groups of members, and built a department at national headquarters that became crucial to the well-being of church families. Over the years, we sponsored many seminars, workshops, articles, and discussion groups.

In sermons and speeches, Rev. and Mrs. Moon gave spiritual guidance and communicated their concerns and desires for each couple to create a family with God at the center of their relationship. Their example provided a role model for a divine partnership that put problems in perspective.

Marriages between partners from different cultures was a reality that added its own kind of stress to relationships. Most of these couples accepted their challenges as an opportunity to resolve differences for the sake of building a peaceful kingdom of heaven on earth and creating and expanding the family of God's children among all people everywhere.

Betsy and I sometimes shed tears as we guided sincere couples over the rocky paths they encountered in marriage and parenthood. As happens in life, there were illnesses, infidelity, differences of opinion, problems with children, financial problems, loss of faith, and even death. A system was set up so that people could confess their mistakes, especially sexual infidelity, receive forgiveness from their spouses, and consider guidance for how they could begin their marriages anew.

Securing Professional Help

Young members, full of enthusiasm and desire to participate in kingdom building, often put aside the baggage they had accumulated and carried with them from earlier years in their lives. As single members living in centers, people could suppress difficult personal issues, believing them to be resolvable through their dedication to the truth of the Divine Principle. With an idealistic faith, many hoped the blessing itself would resolve their problems. They were devastated to find old issues reappearing in the intimacy of marriage and to realize it would take work to clarify and resolve their issues.

Some of the issues involving sex, abuse, abandonment, or mental illness, required skilled professional intervention, but seeking therapies in the secular world was not always acceptable for Asian leaders for whom this was neither familiar nor comfortable. Many church couples also preferred to receive counseling from people who shared their worldview and faith.

I am forever grateful to Patricia, who went on a journey with me to seek therapies that were most helpful, to Lynn, who went to graduate school to obtain a degree in marriage therapy, and to Betsy and Farley, who both took courses to prepare themselves to develop and lead marriage and family workshops for church couples.

Our children grew accustomed to sharing their mother with church members. One of my children commented, "Mom, we should put a sheet over your head when you walk through the lobby of the New Yorker Hotel."

Calling all Women!

I was in a stall in the restroom at national headquarters, making plans for a new project, because it was the only place to get away and think! I had been appointed to lead a One World Crusade mobile team consisting of seventy women. This was not a simple mission for anyone on the team, as most of us were married and some had children. Everyone had daily circumstances to deal with in addition to our new mission.

I was already commuting between our home in Barrytown and New York City to work for the Blessed Family Department. I was also working with Hugh to raise our four children. With this new assignment, I was grateful that Helen, a warm, loving sister from Switzerland, was able and willing to continue to help us care for them.

For the new work to begin in earnest, I needed a long-term vision as well as a plan for each day, and this required two-fold thinking: First, I needed to inspire the members of the team, and then I needed to delegate responsibilities. I asked myself, "What will the team needs be? What are the specific skills of members of the team? Among these women, who can assume leadership roles and who needs special consideration because of personal circumstances?" To meet with each member and find answers to those questions seemed to be a good start. Mary Lou, a person of solid, stable character, became my capable assistant.

The team's mission was to travel from state to state throughout the mid-Atlantic region, meet people, and invite them to hear Divine Principle lectures. If this sounds familiar, that's because it was! Our mission was to bring as many people as possible to embrace the Divine Principle teachings and expand God's kingdom on earth through the marriage blessing. This was only one of many times that individuals and groups would be called to this kind of missionary work.

Two months after our group started working, I reported to headquarters, "We have a unique team, and we are determined to make whatever we are an offering to God for America. We may not always be able to produce a great quantity of work, but we will produce quality results."

My group of sisters were sacrificing much to be on the team. I wanted to make it possible for them to give the best they could, but this would not be the same for each person. Instead of having one standard schedule for everyone, we made individual schedules. "If you can witness for two hours and be successful and happy, you will offer more than you would if you were out all day just marking time," I told them.

On June 1, 1983, I reported to headquarters again: "There are five sisters on maternity leave, fifteen who are pregnant, and one who just gave birth. Fourteen team members are over thirty-five years of age, and eight of them are mothers."

"We purchased a twenty-six-foot motorhome. With a little work, it will be a perfect mobile video center. It was used by a school and is already set up with study desks and a blackboard. Gloria, a member of our team, has a husband who can drive and care for the mobile center."

Triplets

Many of the women had faithful and beautiful hearts. Kathleen was pregnant with triplets due the following month, and she joined the team to make a special offering for her children. What a heart! I told her that she did not need to do anything. Just her being there was enough. However, she expressed her desire to help with fundraising during our Easter stint, selling flowers for at least one day, even if she just sat on a chair on the street. This she did. Soon afterward, she went home to have her babies.

Tears still come to my eyes when I think of the foundation of faith Kathleen made for her three healthy sons. Today, when I hear the names of these three young men, I think of the offering their mother made.

Hearts Won, Lessons Learned

During the next six months of 1983, we traveled to New York City, Albany, Connecticut, New Jersey, Pennsylvania, and Ohio, staying one month in each of the local church centers. Local center leaders may have been surprised at our fluid schedule, but we witnessed daily, taught people who were interested, and left behind new students of the Divine Principle at each place we visited. By sending ahead a small advance team and leaving behind a small follow-up team, we could move more easily and help each state for a longer period.

On June 7, a group of European members joined us, so we split the team, adding European members to both groups. After six months of leading the team, I was assigned to return to my work with blessed families at national headquarters. Franco Ravaglioli, the national leader for our church in Italy, took responsibility for the team in support the American providence.

Living and working with these women on a traveling missionary team was a huge lesson in leadership for me. Previously, I had helped Hugh with his missions and teams. Working without my husband, I realized there needs to be *a head* to plan and *a body* to carry it out. It was difficult to do both, so careful delegation was necessary. I also learned that *doing* will have little success without preparing. By taking the time to prepare and train each person, I could better supervise and support each one.

As a leader, I found it necessary to make three levels of plans: What are we doing in the present? What is the next step? What is the long-term goal? Mapping out and sharing the long-range plan with the team made the daily work easier and more meaningful.

I wrote down my thoughts, and these are the key things I learned through my work on this mission:

1. Include people as part of the process. It is helpful to explain why you make certain decisions or give certain answers.

2. Give people responsibility for what they complain about. If they own their problems, they will find solutions that work.

3. Spend time listening. Even a few moments of attention may make a person's day! Mine too! How often has someone found new life, made a decision, felt understood, or come to grips with a problem when they have felt heard?

4. Meditate. Stop everything and relax. It is good for your health and a time when God can speak.

Our society often debates the need to balance work and family life, and we felt keenly the tension between these two priorities. Throughout the mission, I was aware that everyone on our team was torn between personal family responsibilities and missionary work. It helped to remember that the Moons were dealing with the exact same issues in their own lives. They were parents of a large family who were leading a worldwide mission to bring God's kingdom on earth.

Homemaking—My Joy!

While I was traveling, Hugh was looking for a place near New York City to settle our family, since both of us would be working in the city. In September 1983, we bought our first private home in Dumont, New Jersey, allowing both of us to travel to New York City to work at our national headquarters. Painted a happy yellow, our house had four-bedrooms, a large front yard set back from the street, and a closed-in side porch that Hugh used as an office and library while he worked to complete his doctoral dissertation at Columbia University.

Working in New York City at the Blessed Family Department, I was able to live at home and travel to the city every day. Helen, a faithful church member, still lived in our home and helped take care of our children. Later Noriko lived with us, and she also helped with the children.

I was so happy to live with my family and commute on the bus to New York City to work every day. Homemaking was a pleasure, and Hugh and I set about creating a cozy space for our four children. The children often invited friends over to play and stay overnight. With the house, we inherited a pool table in the basement, and it became a popular spot for the older children and their friends.

Our home was near a Roman Catholic parochial school where we enrolled High, our youngest son, in a full-day kindergarten program. Every day, he walked to school with his preemie cabbage patch kid, *Elwood,* in his backpack. Grandma Spurgin had given him this popular doll for Christmas. One day, he came home from school with a sad face and told me, "Mom, the teacher calls Elwood a doll. I told her that he is my son." One day when I picked him up from school, we passed a statue of Mother Mary, and he asked, "Who's the most important—God, Jesus, or Mother Mary?" At this young age, he was setting his priorities, and it was a good teaching moment. I am always amazed when such a young mind ponders the deeper questions of life.

Shared Sadness

While Hugh was a graduate student at Columbia University, he worked as the executive director of two non-profit organizations founded by Rev. and Mrs. Moon: the International Cultural Foundation and the Professors World Peace Academy. He traveled extensively around America and the world, setting up conferences in many countries where professors could meet to discuss controversial issues in an apolitical, academic setting.

In December 1983, Hugh led a group of PWPA chapter presidents from seventy nations to participate in Rev. Moon's "Victory over Communism" rallies in eight cities in Korea. During this tour, on December 22, Father and Mother Moon received the tragic news that their seventeen-year-old son, Heung Jin, had been critically injured in an automobile accident in Poughkeepsie, New York. On January 2, Heung Jin passed away. Hugh was in Korea with Father and Mother when they learned about the accident. He remembers this shocking moment and their attitude of making this tragedy an offering for God's Providence.

In August 1985, Hugh organized a PWPA conference for Soviet scholars on the *Fall of the Soviet Empire* that was held in Geneva, Switzerland.

Our Children Go to Korea

The Founders of our church had a great interest in education, culture, and the arts. In 1962, they had established the Sun Hwa Arts School, often called the Little Angels School, in Seoul, Korea. During its early years, some of the children of early members of the church in Korea were offered an opportunity to be trained in music, art, and dance. By the 1980s, the school had moved to a beautiful campus in Seoul, Korea. Representing the school and Korea, the Little Angels Children's Folk Ballet dance troupe made goodwill tours worldwide.

The Little Angels School provided an excellent general education for its students. Four of the oldest girls born into European church families were invited to attend the school, where they could learn the Korean language and culture. The following year, Hugh asked Father Moon if our twelve-year-old Andrea could attend. Father's response was, "Yes, but I would also like you to arrange for all American and European second generation blessed children to go there when they reach twelve years of age."

With this new direction, planning began in earnest, and a caring and talented American couple, Mark and Sharon, were sent to Korea to serve as dormitory parents for European and American children enrolled in the school. The program was named the General Orientation Program, and the focus was on students learning the Korean language.

*Sharon and Mark Goodman with the Western students
wearing Korean clothing*

Sharon had been on the Camp Sunrise staff, and I knew she would be an excellent teacher, mentor, and mother figure for our second-generation children. (i.e., children who were born to couples from first generation blessings.). The Japanese church had set up a similar program.

Good-byes

To send our precious first child to the other side of the world pulled at our heartstrings, but Andrea had a mature attitude and saw the decision as an opportunity to be with her friends from Camp Sunrise. On August 15, 1984, fourteen children from America met at JFK airport and boarded a plane for Korea. There were two girls and twelve boys. Hugh prepared everything for the trip and organized all of the passports and tickets. It was natural for him to give all those documents to Andrea to manage during the flight and as they passed through customs and passport control, and she was happy to accept the responsibility.

Parents watched and waved as their children bravely set off into the blue skies that would surround them for the next fifteen hours. They were off to a new adventure. Later, Andrea said, "Mom, because I had everyone's passports and tickets, I had to lead our whole group through customs." Looking back on this, I asked myself, "Were we expecting too much from our young daughter?" But she had managed everything well. Chris, our second child, enrolled in the same program the following year.

Living in a group was fun for them. They entertained each other by creating Saturday evening dramas and skits. They learned the interesting and not so interesting aspects of a different culture. On a shopping trip, they were delighted to find samples of Western food being served in the Lotte Hotel! After eating too many samples, they were kicked out.

Later, our third child, Ameri, took her turn and joined the program when Steve and Noriko Wright were house parents. Our youngest, High, studied for one year in another language study program with three church friends.

Homecoming

Andrea and Chris returned to America to finish high school in Irvington, New York, and Andrea completed advanced studies in textile design and development at the Fashion Institute of Technology (FIT) in New York City. She enjoyed a substantial career in this field before branching out to start her own successful businesses. Chris went to Cornell University, where he graduated summa cum laude. Our multi-talented son attended graduate school in film but decided to become a computer software designer. He has enjoyed stability and independence in his profession.

Our two younger children, Ameri and High, came back to America for high school after spending one year studying in Korea. Ameri (whom we call Ami) has a beautiful voice and often performed in high school and community musical productions. She took vocal lessons with an eye toward a career in music, but art was also an interest, and she chose a career in interior design. Like Andrea, Ami graduated from FIT. Today, she is a designer whose talents are sought after by well-known clients in Manhattan and the Hamptons on Long Island.

After trying different majors and working successfully in theater management and in accounting, our versatile son, High, obtained his degree in logistics management. As a conscientious, diligent, and capable operations manager, he has earned the trust of his employers and is well established in a large firm that makes lasers.

A Tragic Accident

On October 22, 1991, a good friend Takeko Hose (whom we called Tacco) experienced a terrible tragedy, and our family felt the impact of the accident. Tacco and her husband David were one of the seven American couples who had participated with us in the Blessing ceremony in Korea in 1970. They lived near us in Westchester County, New York and our children attended the same schools.

One evening, Tacco was outside her house pruning a fruit tree. After sunset, she continued working in the dark. Her son David Jr. heard the tree branches moving and thought that a deer had emerged from the woods at the edge of their property and was eating the apples.

Having just received a .22 long rifle as a gift for his 15th birthday, David was eager to chase the deer. He grabbed the gun, ran outside and shot into the tree—unaware that his mother was working in the tree after dusk.

Tacco received critical injuries to her lung and spine, leaving her paralyzed for the rest of her life from the waist down. When Hugh arrived at the hospital soon thereafter, he assured the police that it was a tragic accident and that David did not realize it was his mother who was working in the tree.

Tacco later said she felt that God spared her life for the sake of her son who was overcome with grief and guilt—and needed to be consoled and forgiven by his mother. This mother of five children, her husband and her young son have bravely faced a much changed life. On August 21, 2003 our son Chris was blessed in marriage to their daughter, Mary. So we feel a very special connection to their family and empathy for what they experienced.

Tragedy Close to Home

On January 4, 1992 Hugh and I were in Pennsylvania visiting my parents when the phone rang. My mother answered and handed the phone to me. It was Chris. "There has been an accident, and Andrea is in the hospital. I don't know details, but her body was outside the van and her legs were under it. Please come home right away."

In a state of shock, we began the long drive home. We prayed and put Andrea's life in God's hands. I couldn't help but have visions of her with mangled legs. On the way home, we stopped to make phone calls, trying to get more information, but we could not get much of a response. (In those days we did not have mobile phones.) At least we knew Andrea was alive.

Four hours later, we were ushered into Andrea's hospital room. She greeted us, saying she was okay, but she looked as though she had been through an ordeal. The whites of her eyes were completely red, she was badly bruised, and her shoulder was painful. We embraced her and prayed with her. Then, with tears in her eyes, she told us that David, the son of our dear friends,

Edwin and Marie Ang, may have been killed in the accident. She was very worried about him and his family. Indeed, at just 18 years of age, this beautiful young man had lost his life. How could this have happened?

Andrea and a group of her friends had been at a church workshop. It was a rainy evening, and many of them decided to go to a movie. They borrowed a fifteen-seat van from the workshop and twenty-two kids crammed into it. Rounding a curve, the driver lost control, and the van rolled over twice. Three of the young people were hurled out of the van. Most of the young passengers escaped with minor injuries such as bruises, cuts, and scratches.

David's death was a shocking, sobering event for everyone. The news deeply saddened many in the church because the Ang family were well-known and David much beloved. He was a handsome, bright, and loving young man on the brink of his adult life. His loss was profound for his family and all who knew him.

We were grateful that Andrea survived. Chris had decided not to go, feeling that loading the van so full was dangerous. Our fourteen-year-old Ameri was also in the van. Although she was not hurt, watching the ambulance pick up David and Andrea had been a traumatic experience. Not knowing what had happened to them, and fearing the worst, she went to all three hospitals in Westchester County where the injured were taken, but she could not find her sister. When we finally connected with Ameri, she was frantic. Whenever I think of this tragedy, my heart still wants to reach out and comfort my children and hold them safely in my arms.

Accepting Vulnerability

As parents, we realized there was a need for greater supervision of the activities of our teenaged children. No longer would we naïvely believe that our children or any of us were invincible in God's hands. In our young church, we may have been idealistic to a fault, but with the loss of both Heung Jin and David, we had to face the fact that we were as vulnerable to the challenges and sorrows of life as anyone.

Intimacy with God

Working with couples in the Blessed Family Department and with the women on my bus team gave me greater awareness of the problems people encounter in family life. As I watched my children grow up, I grew with them. With the loss of two precious young lives and the impairment of a mother's life, I felt deep sorrow, but also the grace of God's personal love and comfort. With these experiences, I gained greater spiritual maturity. I understood, whatever happened, that God would be there for us.

CHAPTER 10

Family Connections

More than ever, I wanted to maintain a close and meaningful relationship with the children, but this was not a new idea for me. From the time Andrea was born, I had looked for ways to connect, believing this was an important part of parenting. Children are always in need of something to do, and when they say they are bored, it can mean they are feeling disconnected. As parents, we may respond by arranging entertaining activities for them, sometimes at no small expense. But it is in daily interactions that we can find unique opportunities to stay connected.

Kid Connections

When our children were in middle school, several families in the church decided to take turns hosting our children in a variety of groups so they could play together, and this became a pattern. Every weekend, we made trips to each other's homes. The Jones, Hose, Spurgin, and Schauffler families often spent weekends together in one combination or another. Each family hosted one of four groups: older girls, older boys, younger girls, or younger boys.

The kids loved it!

Not only were the kids happy, but the parents found it more fun to entertain them in groups of similar ages. Our children had sometimes encountered expressions of animosity toward the Unification Church in the media or at school. Spending time with each other and with parents of their friends meant they were in a safe space. They were comfortable with each other because they could be completely free.

Clean-up Connections

Early in my career as a mother, I began finding things to do with the children to keep them occupied, entertained, and connected with each other and with me. That often meant looking at things I had to do and including them. We often made games out of chores that had to be done.

Having grown up in a large family, I had learned to view common chores as a joyful experience. Picking up toys every evening before bedtime was a great game, and all the kids in our family took part. We devised a special way to pick up our most popular toy, Legos, at the end of the day. We each had our own little bucket, and we counted the Legos as we picked them up. This had the added benefit of teaching the youngest to count! Even the baby proudly held up his bucket with a few legos in it, and said, "I got 100!" He had the idea, anyway.

As our children grew older, I sought ways to continue making connections with them in simple ways. We crawled into bed together at night and read all the books in the series, *Little House on the Prairie.* Those are still great memories for us. Our eldest daughter, Andrea, became a genius at the age of nine in getting her stubborn little brother to cooperate. Once, when High was resisting putting on his clothes, I was frustrated. There was a disconnect. Andrea said, "Mom, let me try." With great calm, she held up the pant legs and said, "We're going to watch the seeds grow. See, I'm dropping a seed into the leg. Now give me your foot and watch it come out." With great delight, he stopped resisting and sent his little foot down a pant leg until it peeked through. After that, the socks and shoes were no problem. Andrea had found a way to connect with High, and I marveled at my daughter's creativity!

Saturday mornings were cleaning time at our house. Doing this job together was fun, and it made the time pass quickly. I gave each child a grocery sack and sent them to different rooms to pick up everything that did not belong on the floor, put it in the sack, and bring it to me. I sat at the kitchen table as the sacks came in filled with pieces of paper, dirty socks, pennies, pins, game pieces, pencils, and other odds and ends. We dumped the sacks and sat around the table sorting the contents and putting everything away. This made vacuuming the floor a cinch.

At other times, each child received a small bucket of soapy water and a sponge and went throughout the house wiping off fingerprints. Years later, as a high school principal, I had the students do the same thing as part of end-of-the-year cleaning. Breaking a large job into small tasks makes work easier for all of us.

Puzzle Connections

As our children became teenagers, I found new ways to connect. We all enjoyed jigsaw puzzles. Sometimes I set out a card table with a puzzle. When they came home from school or a social activity, they found me quietly working on it. They were drawn to insert a few pieces, and this activity would turn into a time of quality connection. Working on a puzzle together provided a great time to talk.

During my father-in-law's final days, his children gathered in his home. It was a time to be together, but there was also a sense of waiting. No one was comfortable to leave the house for any length of time. I brought a puzzle and set it up on a card table close to Grandpa's bed. Children and grandchildren stopped by in small groups and worked on sections of the puzzle. It gave us something to do, a way to have quiet conversations, and an opportunity to just be present with Grandpa.

Tentative Connections

Teenaged boys are not known to seek their mother's advice, and mine were no exception. At one point, I decided to pay my sixteen-year-old son to give my tired shoulders a five-minute massage every evening. He always needed a little money, and I always liked a little massage, so it was a point of connection! Sometimes we traded, and I gave him a foot massage. This acceptable physical connection could result in our having a conversation—or not.

Community Connections

When my son Chris was in high school, we lived in Irvington, New York. A neighboring family had a child with cerebral palsy, and they were helping her with a special process called patterning, where volunteers moved the child's arms and legs to simulate a crawling pattern. It was believed that doing this every day could stimulate development of the brain.

I wanted our children to learn to serve others, so I asked Chris if he would like to volunteer for this special hands-on service. He agreed, and for two years he served the family in this way. I was so proud of him for taking this task seriously and doing it consistently. He will never forget the experience, and the child's parents still express their gratitude to him.

Spiritual Connections

Children can make deep spiritual connections, and their questions reflect that. It would be a shame to miss such moments. Once Chris and Andrea, at five and six years old, were holding an incredible discussion as I was driving. They asked me, "Mom, is God inside or outside the world?" I was amazed. It was a profound theological question! I said, "Why don't you tell me what you think?" After a long discussion, they announced they had the answer. With great fascination, I waited for it. "We decided God cannot be in the world, because there is evil in the world, so he must be outside the world, but he can still live in people's hearts."

More than once, Chris asked, "Who is God's mother?" It was a mystery for which neither of us had an answer.

Trip Connections

Hugh and I knew that when we took occasional family trips, we would always have memories we could keep as a reference. Once, I took the older children to Disney World in Orlando, Florida. Later Hugh took Andrea and the younger children there, while Chris was in Korea. Frequently, we visited my family in Lancaster County, Pennsylvania.

Hugh's parents were always supportive of our work.
Here they were enjoying their family at the ranch.

Our trips to St. Louis, Missouri, were among the most memorable. Hugh's uncle Pete owned a 2,700 acre ranch in Branson, Missouri, and Hugh's parents arranged for their family to spend a week or more there each summer. Hugh's cousins and their families were often there with us. Shared experiences like singing around campfires, playing sports, riding horses, and canoeing helped us forge rich relationships that continue to the present day. Every three years, one of the cousins still hosts a reunion attended by forty or more family members. We have gathered in St. Louis, San Diego, Palm Springs, Seattle, New Paltz, NY, and Clermont, FL.

Family fun at the ranch created connections that resulted in family reunions every three years up until the present day.

There was never much time or money to take extensive pleasure trips, but the trips we did take have created memories that will last forever and help to keep alive our connections with each other.

Written Connections

Even though Hugh and I worked on many different missions and traveled frequently, our relationships with each other and with our children remained central to our hearts and the most important aspect of our lives. We did what we could to spend quality time with our children and connect with them in meaningful ways, even though our missions were not always easy for them to understand. When we traveled, although they were cared for either by a live-in babysitter or by care givers in a church nursery, we always missed our precious children.

During those travels, I kept a journal for each child, each page filled with love and tears. Sadly, my bag was stolen at an airport, and those irreplaceable journals were lost. I have tried to rewrite one for each child, but I haven't been able to convey what I was feeling at the time I was writing the original journals. If only I can find a way to tell them how much I loved them, how much I missed them, and how it broke my heart to be away from them.

Several years ago, my daughter-in-law gave me a book titled *Grandma, Tell Me Your Story*. Its pages required me to record key events of my life for her children, my two grandsons. The book includes questions like, "What have you learned that you want to pass on to me?" I have been writing in that book and will make a copy for each grandchild.

By 2008, the kids were grown. With Hugh, they planned and hosted a seventieth birthday party for me with more than one hundred family members and friends. The children presented me with a beautiful gift—a book they had compiled and printed. It contained wonderful pictures of our family, but most meaningful to me were the words they wrote about our life together.

Andrea reflected on my service to others with gracious observations and fond memories of a trip taken by three generations of Spurgin women:

> *Mom,*
> *Growing up, we had to share you with many.*
> *Somehow, you had room in your heart for all:*
> *mom to many*
> *comforter of broken spirits*
> *counselor to failed marriages*
> *guide to the lost*
> *rescuer to the hurt*
> *teacher to the unruly*

There were many days that we spent apart, but it was easier knowing that we were always in your heart. My fondest memory is our trip up the East Coast with Grandma. We enjoyed the changing foliage, building puzzles, shopping, and each other. We had no deadline or destination and just enjoyed the moment. I look forward to many more special moments together.

Love, Andrea

Chris recalled a time of making connections as an adult:

10 years ago, straight out of college, I came to Connecticut and had the opportunity to become reacquainted with you and Dad. Over these last years, I have learned that we can talk and laugh easily. To love someone is to accept them fully, and that's what I feel between us. Simply put, I enjoy your company immensely. No matter where you and Dad are or Mary and I may go in the coming years, I will always look to the last decades as a time I grew to understand you. I can say without reservation that not only are you a great parent, you are a great friend.

Love, Chris

Ameri recognized some bumpy times with appreciation:

I am so happy that I have a chance to write my appreciation for you in a letter. There are so many opportunities to tell you how much I love you but those moments always seem to pass. I can't express in words what you give to me without even knowing it. You are doing an amazing job being my mom, and I don't think I tell you enough. I admit I was trouble at times in the past but look at it this way: I kept it interesting for you. I love you very much and I think you are a keeper!

Love, Ami

High offered his love and support:

From the pitter-patter of feet to the stumps in anger, you have persevered through it all. I thank you for the hope and strength you have given us. When all seemed lost, you have been there for all of us. We love you mom. You have allowed love to dwell in our home throughout all our childhood until this current day. You were successful in raising four beautiful children. We wish all the happiness in the world to you. Enjoy this new chapter in your life. Just know that all of us are here to help in any way possible.

Love, High

I feel inspired to include the concluding pages written by Chris. With his own sense of humor and artistry with words, he captured many of the moments of my life:

Born a Mennonite farmer's daughter in Pennsylvania Dutch country, she wore her curly brown hair in a white bonnet. The women in the family dressed in plain calico dresses and the men in black slacks and white shirts. They drove small German cars with the chrome bumpers painted black and attended Sunday service in a church with knotty pine floorboards and their white walls—men on one side and women on the other. They ate sweet potatoes and stew and shoofly pie.

At 21 years old, standing just over 5 feet tall give or take one inch of hair, she left home. She'd never tasted wine. She'd never seen a movie. She'd never gone to high school. She had traveled with migrant workers in Florida. She worked her way through college and drove a VW bug named Susie up to New York for graduate school. She had a pure, sweet smile, and was popular among the rebels of the bonnet—wearing crowd.

In graduate school, she found something she wasn't exactly looking for—a religion called the Unification Church. Here she was introduced to a new vocabulary: she paid indemnity by taking cold showers, sang holy songs during early Sunday pledge services in Belvedere, witnessed to new members in the IOWC, and counseled the Cained-out members. Did you get all that?

Her husband was a lean man from Indiana who wore tan suits, horn-rimmed glasses, and faux-fur black hats in the winter. She was short and gregarious; he was tall and reserved. His skin turned red in the sun; she was permanently roasted a walnut brown. They were married along with 776 other couples standing in alternating rows of dark suits and white dresses. They bought their first home in Minnesota [in reality in New Jersey], and all in all her husband turned out to be a fine fellow. She loved him even though to this day he clutters the coffee table with newspapers.

The first years of marriage were grand times. Then the children came.

The first child looked like an old man at birth. She was born serious and righteous like her father. The second had a permanent grin on his face, irreverent like his great-grandfather committed to a mental hospital. The third was a busy little Koala, just like her mother, and she was friends with everyone. The fourth was a preemie, born the size of a sock monkey, and he spent his first years grunting instead of speaking. Eventually he learned to speak.

In the early years, the children ruled the household. They set the bedtime and hired and fired the babysitters. The children were curiously immune to spankings—nothing could harm their kryptonite little bottoms. Mother cooked up some hearty meals: spaghetti and meatballs and surprise casserole, which was cheese on top of mashed potatoes on top of last night's leftovers. At the end of every day, she put them to sleep with her soothing voice as she read the Little House on the Prairie books.

She was more than a mother—she was a leader, philosopher, new age guru and cosmopolitan globetrotter. Decked out in her periwinkle polyester pant suit, she traveled to India, China, Brazil, Russia, North Korea and other countries, spreading a message of peace. A man in Egypt once offered to give her husband 100 camels in exchange for her to join him as his fourth wife. This was not a bad deal at the time, far above the market rate for a wife in Egypt.

But for all her speeches and traveling, she found comfort at home working on projects. She invented the Ami doll—it had a round head like the real Ami.—And she edited a quarterly journal. She also had magic powers: she spiritually sent nutrients to her husband by putting a magnet on top of vitamins and a picture of her husband. However, the magic backfired when she discovered her eldest son put the magnet on top of her checkbook and a picture of himself, surreptitiously transmitting her bank account to himself.

Over the years, the children have grown and have come to appreciate their mother's warmth all the more. She and her husband now run a high school in Connecticut, and in case you're wondering, she's the boss. One day she may retire. She'll tend her garden, build water fountains for friends and use up all her timeshare days in the Poconos.

We wouldn't trade our mother for a thousand camels. (For a thousand camels, we might trade her and then hire a bounty hunter to get her back.) Yes, everyone loves our mother, and we are all very proud of her.

In a book that the children made a few years later, for Hugh's seventieth birthday, they wrote these descriptions of themselves:

*First, there was the calm, practical **Capricorn** who looked like her daddy. Yes, that would be the grounded, reliable, and loyal traditionalist who followed all the rules.*

Then of course there was the free-thinking, inquisitive

Aquarius—*idealistic and unconventional. The one that marched to the beat of a different drummer and resisted all conventions and rules.*

Add to the mix, the free-spirited **Sagittarius**—*cheerful, spontaneous, and adaptable. With a skip in her step and a song on her lips.*

Then, last but not least, the affectionate Aries preemie, who was really meant to be a **Taurus**—*loyal, passionate, stubborn, optimistic, and loving. The youngest of the bunch does not rock the boat.*

Our adult children with their spouses: Andrea and Tim Porter, Chris and Mary Spurgin, Ameri and Mike, and High and Kym Spurgin

I can only conclude that our efforts to stay connected with our children were successful. Giving credit where credit is due, the children themselves have made consistent efforts to connect with us and with each other. Today they are loving and supportive toward their parents, siblings, spouses, and their own children. We all placed value on staying connected, and our investments have paid off! It is always a great joy to see our children find love with a life partner, bringing security and stability to their lives and the added blessing of grandchildren for us. Each of our children found love and marriage in their own way.

CHAPTER 11

Frontline of History

Historic moments are those likely to change the course of history or to stand out as major events in history. Growing up in a provincial setting in my Mennonite community, I could never have imagined that I would be present at just such a moment.

The Berlin Wall

The date was November 9, 1989. I was watching the news on TV when there was an urgent announcement: The Berlin wall was coming down! I watched in amazement as people demolished it with sledgehammers. They were climbing through the rubble from East Germany to West Germany. This wall, separating communism from democracy in Germany was coming down before my eyes and the eyes of the world. I was moved to tears as I saw West Berliners welcome East Berliners to freedom. What a moment! Earlier that year, Hyo Jin, the eldest of the fourteen Moon children, had led a team of youth to pray at the Berlin wall.

Watching on television the Berlin wall being destroyed was a powerful moment. Another historical moment was much more powerful when two years later, I was in Lithuania during a coup in the Soviet Union.

The Collapse of the Soviet Union

In 1991, things were changing rapidly in the former Soviet Union. As communism loosened its grip, the atmosphere was right for educating youth to religious values and a new way of life. Our church viewed this as an opportunity to step into a vacuum by creating the International Educational Foundation. Without religious terminology, literature was produced by the IEF that was focused on an understanding of human spirituality, moral values, democratic ideals and the value of freedom. During the summer of 1991, teams of American Unificationists traveled into the former Soviet Union to educate youth about democracy and spiritual values. They were invited to spend 40 days teaching at one of the many newly established youth education workshops. Responding to this call, I went to Lithuania.

In August 1991, after spending a few days in Latvia, I arrived in Lithuania to help staff a workshop to be hosted in classrooms and dormitories on the campus of an agricultural college in Atlantis. It was exciting to work with students who had just transitioned from a tight communist system to one that was offering greater freedom. They were happy to share their experiences.

One day I went shopping to buy gifts for people back home, and I was surprised to see that the store had very few items. To buy something, one had to go through about five steps with a different person at each station. When I commented to a student that it seemed they did not want to sell the items to me, the student told me this was indeed the case. Accustomed to high-pressure advertising and the free market system, I was almost embarrassed to learn that products were tightly controlled, and I was doing them no favor by making purchases.

I had been advised to bring small gifts from America for my team members, and someone suggested that small solar-powered pocket calculators would be valued. At the end of the workshop, I gave each team member one of the calculators I had brought. They gratefully received them and felt that I had given them a special gift, even though in America they were not expensive.

After I returned home, Arkadiy, a young medical student who was interested in music, sent me a letter saying he hoped I did not mind that he had traded the calculator for a guitar. He was so happy to own a guitar, and he even drew a picture of it with my name written on it. One never knows the impact of a small gift.

Sightseeing in Lithuania with some of the students attending our workshop.

Coup in the Soviet Union

While I was still in Lithuania, a major event occurred, and our situation changed dramatically. An excerpt from my journal on Monday morning tells the story:

We awakened to the news that there was a military coup in Moscow. Gorbachev was ousted and hardline communists in the military have seized power. The VP, a hardline communist, is in charge, and Gorbachev is reported to be too ill to hold office. Moscow is at the center of the action.

Here we were in rural Lithuania, with over a hundred students and thirty-five staff members. We heard the news of the coup with numbing shock. My first thoughts were, "What do we do with the students? Will they experience punishment for associating with us?" Neither they nor we had protection now, for we had been given permission to hold the workshops by the Gorbachev government.

Fear crept through me. Would I have to stay a long time? What about my husband and children? Would I ever see them again? I had visions of walking through countries and crossing blockaded borders and of Lithuania rebelling and the Soviet military invading. I thought of the possibility of imprisonment. Might we go to prison because we were Unification Church members and anti-Communists? Would I be willing to die here? Would I have a choice?

I prayed and began to feel a deep peace and then a sense of gratitude that I was in Lithuania at that specific historic moment. "*It is a blessing,*" I thought. "I do not want to be anywhere else right now. I am here for these special students."

The students themselves had become quiet and pensive. Some were depressed, some felt resigned, and others helpless. They talked of having to go to the army or collective farms. They wanted to call home, but we were cut off completely from the outside world. There were no phones and no radios. It was a dark and dreary day.

Our workshop leaders decided to report whatever news they could get and then proceed with our regular lecture schedule. The students calmed down and waited.

The staff had a special prayer room where we offered daily prayers and devotions for the success of the workshop. I was inspired to suggest that we open our doors and invite the students to come in and pray with us. I knew we had to expand our own thinking. Lithuania was the students' country, and they should have the opportunity to pray. This was a moment for us to teach by example.

On the wall, we put up a map of the Soviet Union countries. We lit candles, put on classical religious music, and invited anyone who wanted to come in to sing, meditate, and pray together. A few students cautiously ventured in. Gradually, more joined us.

We told the students we would stay with them as long as we could, and we wanted them to receive as much as we could offer. Some talked of having secret meetings when they returned to Moscow and St. Petersburg (then Leningrad).

While we had no phones, radios, or televisions, we received additional news from a church missionary who visited.

Tuesday evening: *The news sounds bad. There were tanks in Moscow. People have been killed. There were also tanks in the Baltics. Communications were taken over.*

We went to bed with heavy hearts, but we were not losing hope entirely. Not everyone was falling in line in Moscow. Yeltsin was gaining support, and people were resisting the military. Could there be a war? At the same time, we felt the situation could not last long. Maybe evil was rearing its ugly head one last time. After this, communism might be eradicated forever. What would tomorrow bring?

Wednesday morning: *Jack and Peter* [Unification Church missionary leaders in Russia] *spoke to our group, encouraging us to keep going and to believe that the situation in Moscow will last for only a short time.*

Invisible Value of Prayer

The crisis was over! We completed our forty-day workshop without interference, and I returned home to gratefully join my husband and children in Pennsylvania.

A short time later, Hugh visited a spiritual medium who was going to give him a reading, and I went with him. Soon after we arrived, the medium said, "This is most unusual. There are many here from the other side requesting to bring a message to Nora. They are dressed like Eastern Orthodox priests. I have no idea why they are here, but they are eager to meet Nora." Then the medium invited me into the room with Hugh, and he began to give a reading for both of us. He said, "This strong presence of the spirit world is here to thank you, Nora, for the prayers, they say."

I was touched by this message. The medium we visited had no idea that I had been in Lithuania and Russia, and he certainly did not know about the special prayers we had said with the Soviet students.

For me, this was a powerful confirmation that we should act on our inspirations, as even a small act can bring positive repercussions and results. Receiving the gratitude of those faithful who had passed over dressed in the traditional religious garb of Russia and Lithuania was deeply meaningful.

A Giant Leap toward Peace

As I look back at the special points of connection in my missionary experience, this one was different. Most of my mission work involved witnessing, teaching, counseling, and administrative tasks, and so did this one, but it was unique. Like other missions, this brief visit to Lithuania was filled with internal meaning, the energy of working closely with other members, and the joy of seeing new people finding their own closer connection with God. More than many other missions, however, it brought us to a turning point in history.

The coup would fail, and a sea change would happen in the world, including the breakup of the Soviet Union. Democracy would surge at first and then falter under a powerful old-style leader, but the Cold War seemed over. Taking the long view, it is still hard to see a day when all people join hands as one family under God, but at that moment in time, we felt like we were entering a new era of hope for world peace.

Now, thirty years later I am watching Putin's invasion of Ukraine. It brings my mind back to the coup that I had experienced. I think specifically of the Ukrainian students who studied with us in Lithuania and pray that they and their friends may remain free from authoritarian rule.

CHAPTER 12

Women for World Peace

I was home safe in the United States and back at my job as director of the Blessed Family Department. I really enjoyed the work and felt I could contribute to a cause that mattered to individuals, families, and the church as a whole. We had our own home in New Jersey, and the children were doing well. Hugh was working as vice president of the American Church. Our lives seemed to have entered a stable period. Andrea had graduated from Fashion Institute of Technology and had taken a textile design job in New York City.

On the surface of things, we seemed to be moving toward peace in the world, in our professional lives, and in our family. I didn't know what was coming, but I was on the brink of another turning point.

Financial Uncertainty

Supporting our family while working on full-time church missions required careful planning. When we first joined the church in the late 60s, we had professional jobs with rather good salaries. During the years when we were full-time missionaries, we often lived in church centers with single members. When working at headquarters, we received small stipends and sometimes lived in church-supported facilities. When Hugh was working on a PhD, he received a church scholarship. Anytime we were not working on a church mission or in a church-related educational program, we needed to independently produce our own income, as most people do.

My parents owned two farms, but as my father got older, his sons were no longer at home to help with farm work. Along a country road bordering our farm, he owned beautiful property that could be used for homebuilding. There was a demand for housing in the area, and my father received offers, so he decided to sell some of his property and divide the proceeds among his nine children.

My relatives at a luncheon after my father's funeral in 2005

My mother had passed away from cancer at the age of fifty-eight, and my father realized the fragility of life. He wanted to give his children part of their inheritance at a time when they had young families and might be most in need of it. Thus, we occasionally received an inheritance check that was much welcomed. Such checks would sometimes miraculously appear at a time when we needed to buy a car or make a large purchase. Later, we received an inheritance from Hugh's parents' estate, as well as a final inheritance check from my father's estate. We will always be grateful for the help of our parents.

Abrupt Change

In August 1991, our Founders encouraged members to move to their hometowns to restore and solidify relationships with family, relatives, and friends. Called Hometown Providence, this was an opportunity to renew old acquaintances and care for aging parents.

When this plan was announced, Hugh and I were both working at national headquarters in missions that suited our training, skills, and abilities. With this new providence the Korean leader of our church in America decided to reduce costs and staff at headquarters. One day he announced that our departments will be closed. He then suggested that we go to our hometown.

Hugh and I understood and appreciated Father Moon's direction to build bridges in our hometowns, but we were both deeply committed to the work that we had been doing. My faith and commitment were never more tested than at that moment. It was hard to find peace about this abrupt change.

With no jobs and with children who were in high school and college, we did some fancy financial footwork to make ends meet until we could find jobs. We rented our house and moved into a small apartment. Hugh researched potential jobs in Indiana and Pennsylvania, and I taught English to Japanese women. In the process, we declared bankruptcy, did a short sale on our house and moved to Pennsylvania near my home where I got a job as a psychiatric consultant in a nursing home. Hugh got a job at the *Washington Golf Monthly*, a publication of the *Washington Times* newspaper that is owned by the church.

Finally, we settled into our new situation, but it wouldn't be long before I was called to do a new project and our lives changed again.

Peace Initiative

An April rain was pouring as Mother Moon spoke from under an umbrella in the Seoul Olympic Stadium. A crowd of 160,000 women from seven countries listened attentively. She shared her vision of the significant role of women in global peacemaking. That day, on April 6, 1992, she proclaimed the era of women and inaugurated the Women's Federation for World Peace International, or WFWP.

I was asked to travel to Korea to help prepare couples from the Middle East for their international blessing in Seoul, and I had received a request from the Korean leader in America, Rev. Zin Moon Kim, to represent American women at the event where Mother Moon was speaking. Seated under my own umbrella near the front of this huge crowd of women, I observed her passionate call for a worldwide network of women leaders to join her on the path to world service and peace.

Peace Building in America

Upon my return home in May 1992, I was asked to take on the leadership of the newly inaugurated WFWP in America as its president. At that point, I received a title, but there was no organization! I wondered how I would go about building one.

With the help of the church structure and membership, women from throughout America stepped up with enthusiasm to take roles as chairpersons of WFWP groups at state and regional levels. They invested their talents, skills, creativity, and often-untapped energy to establish local chapters as well. At the national headquarters, Betsy Jones and several women representing the Japanese and Korean women in America were assigned as vice presidents.

We created an organizational chart and a newsletter to share the efforts and ideas of our nationwide network. Without any church funding, we created a membership organization with monthly dues to support our simple structure and activities. With the help of staff at headquarters, we set up a 501 (c) (3) non-profit organization. At first, we had modest ambitions for WFWP in America, but the organization was to take on a life of its own.

When Mother Moon completed her speaking tour in Japan and Korea, she turned her attention to America, announcing an eight-city speaking tour to begin in October 1992. In each city, influential women heard her message. She chose to speak in English, and she diligently practiced her speech to perfect her delivery. Three WFWP leaders traveled with her on the tour: Josette served as the MC, Betsy gave the call to action, and I introduced Mother Moon to the audience. The tour stirred things up among church women and other women in America, and WFWP became a more viable organization. Nearly four years later in May 1997, WFWP International was granted NGO general consultative status with the Economic and Social Council, ECOSOC, at the United Nations. Linda, one of my staff members at our headquarters worked diligently for nearly a year on the application for this prestigious recognition. She researched reports from WFWP worldwide on the activities of national and local WFWP organizations and their membership.

Peace Building Abroad

After the speaking tour in America, Mother Moon took her tour to England, Germany, Austria, France, Italy, Russia, and China. Again, I traveled with her, as did the WFWP leaders of European nations. It was a great opportunity for international bonding. By this time, women of our church in Europe were initiating WFWP organizations in their respective nations. Everywhere, women in the church were eager to take responsibility for an organization that called out their leadership energies.

American church members had been working in Russia for many years.

Hence, when the tour arrived in Moscow church women had already created a WFWP organization there. We got off to a bumpy start in obtaining a venue, but the women of WFWP in Russia helped with preparations and we held a successful event. I was grateful to see women in every country stfep up to lay the foundation for this powerful work.

After each speech, members gathered around Mother Moon while she called her husband in New York to share how things had gone. From their respective locations, they chatted over the phone. In unison, they would cut a celebration cake and make eating sounds over the phone. Only then did Mother relax. For me, those were sweet moments. We could enjoy their phone conversations, celebrate with them, and see another side of their lives.

After speaking in each nation, Mother Moon spoke by phone to her husband who was in America. It was a joy to see her relax and enjoy the conversation.

Peace Efforts in China

The speech in China presented challenges. As we walked through Tiananmen Square in 1992, I thought of the blood shed on that very spot, not long before, in 1990. Then we walked into a beautiful hall, the Great Hall of the People. We were dressed as we thought appropriate for the venue, and Mrs. Moon was wearing a beautiful suit with gold threads in the fabric, but the Chinese women were dressed in casual pants and sweaters, making us feel a bit overdressed.

The Chinese Communist Party had initially refused to grant us a permit for the speech. They had reviewed the script of the speech and rejected it. After meeting and negotiating with the son of Deng Xiaoping, the paramount leader, we were finally allowed to speak at a meeting of the All-China Women's Federation, an organization not associated with WFWP. Every woman in China was a member, which meant we might have wide exposure. Mother Moon bravely gave her original talk, which contained many references to God. This created a little stir in the audience, but she was able to complete the speech. Her significant charm helped.

Sisterhood Ceremonies in America

In 1994, Father and Mother Moon called a meeting with Motoko Sugiyama (president of WFWP in Japan), myself and Betsy. They explained that Japanese women had traveled to Korea where they held a ceremony in which individual Japanese and Korean women met with each other to form sisterhood pairs. For many, this had been a deeply moving experience.

Korean women carried pain in their hearts because of abuse inflicted by Japanese men during a forty-year period when Japan occupied Korea. The Japanese and Korean sisters cried in each other's arms as they repented and forgave in turn. They felt liberated and healed from the historical resentment they had inherited from the experiences of prior generations.

In the United States, there was resentment in the hearts of Americans who had lost loved ones at Pearl Harbor and elsewhere during World War II. The Moons wanted to make a ceremony in America to address that issue. "Can you prepare 500 American women to attend a sisterhood ceremony with Japanese women?" they asked me.

It was a daunting but happy task. What a wonderful opportunity to create a vehicle to bring healing and peace to women of these two nations! Father Moon's heart had an even deeper purpose. He believed the Japanese women would bring with them the spirit of their newly acquired Korean sisters, thus connecting them to American women. The hearts of the women of all three nations would be united, creating a deeper flow of harmony between our three nations and a foundation for world peace.

The Bridge of Peace

Mr. Douglas Joo, president of the *Washington Times* newspaper, was commissioned to help our fledgling WFWP organization. I wanted to create a ceremony that would touch the hearts of women, and in meetings with Mr. Joo and our combined staffs, we hashed out a plan. Tomiko, a member of Mr. Joo's staff, provided many ideas from a Japanese perspective. Yoko, a member of the WFWP staff, served as a mediator with the Japanese participants.

On the stage in the hotel rooms where we held our conferences, we created a bridge with a set of stairs in the center of the bridge leading down to the stage. With the powerful song, "Let There Be Peace on Earth," playing in the background, pairs of Japanese and American women walked from each side of the bridge toward the center. They bowed to each other halfway, representing their offering of repentance and forgiveness and then continued toward the center. When they reached each other, they embraced and turned to face the audience. They raised their clasped hands and descended the stairs surrounded by the applause of seated Japanese and American women. There were many tears as each international pair crossed the bridge and pledged friendship as sisters.

I had wanted to create a ceremony that would touch the hearts of women, and my wish came true. The Bridge of Peace became a signature project of WFWP and a beautiful symbol of sisterhood. But it was more than that. Time and time again, we experienced these precious bridge crossings as acts of authentic healing. I can still see the faces and feel the sincerity of the participants. Thousands of women from all over the world crossed that bridge. In our faith, symbolic acts by sincere individuals can exert great spiritual power in heaven and earth, potentially affecting the course of history. Thinking of the Bridge of Peace ceremonies always makes my heart sing.

Peace at Home

When I was not traveling with Mother Moon's various tours, I was in Washington four days on the weekend each week for WFWP sisterhood ceremonies. I returned to Pennsylvania one day for my part-time job as a psychiatric consultant in a nursing home and commuted to New York City to work there for two additional days. Physically it was a grueling schedule, and it was challenging to work with three major church leaders and their sometimes-competing priorities. Most of all, there was the ever-present heart-tug of wanting to spend more time with my family.

When we started Bridge of Peace ceremonies with Japanese and American women, I arranged with Motoko Sugiyama, the president of WFWP in Japan, for her two daughters, Keikoh and Keimei, to live with our family in Reading, Pennsylvania. This worked out well for both families, and it was helpful to us financially. The Sugiyama girls could go to high school with Ameri and High, providing valuable companionship and support for all four teenagers.

With their typical resilience, my children seemed to adjust well to our unusual commuting patterns. Sometimes Hugh and I came home to a house ringing with music and laughter. They all enjoyed drama, and all of them had roles in their school plays. Once I caught Keimei with a big Cheshire cat grin on her face, and when I asked her why she was smiling, she said, "Our house is so fun!"

Prominent Friends of Peace

The *Washington Times* had a working relationship with many political leaders. Through these relationships, women of influence were invited to speak and participate in the Bridge of Peace Ceremonies, increasing the visibility of our events. Former Canadian Prime Minister Brian Mulrony spoke and former first lady Mila Pivnicki participated. Former President George H.W. Bush and former first lady Barbara Bush were speakers at several events, and Barbara crossed the bridge with Motoko Sugiyama. After getting to know them through the Bridge of Peace events, I gained a deep respect for the Bush family, as they represented positive American values.

Journal Entry, December 2018:

> *Today George Bush died. As I listened to the news documenting this great man of character and integrity, I am reminded of my own interaction with him and Barbara. It began when the Bushes were invited to speak and cross the Bridge of Peace at our sisterhood ceremonies. I remember sitting beside President Bush when Barbara crossed the bridge with Motoko Sugiyama, president of WFWP, Japan. President Bush leaned over with tears sparkling in his eyes, and said, "If we would have done this 50 years ago, we may have prevented a war." That war, World War II, was very personal to him, as at 18 years of age, he had enlisted and served as a naval aviator.*

Later, they were invited to speak in Japan. Mrs. Sugiyama and I accompanied them to the WFWP event at the Tokyo Dome. I remember getting off the elevator in a hotel in Tokyo to be warmly greeted by the Bushes by name. They understood WFWP's mission and remained friends of WFWP and of mine. For me, this was a most humbling experience, but I realized this was for the sake of God's work. I will always value the relationship with them, because I know they both recognized, respected, and valued the depth of the work of our movement in peacemaking.

Meeting with former President George H.W. and First Lady Barbara Bush in Tokyo, Japan where they spoke in the Tokyo Dome.

The Bushes were deeply moved by the Bridge of Peace Ceremonies.

The Bushes pose with attendees of a Bridge of Peace sisterhood ceremony.

A Worldwide Source of Harmony

The Bridge of Peace ceremonies generated one remarkable story after another. An older African American woman joined a young Japanese woman in a sisterhood walk. Both were so moved by their experience that they wiped the tears from their eyes with the same handkerchief, offered by the Japanese sister. At the end of the ceremony, the Japanese sister gave the handkerchief to her American sister to keep.

When she returned home, the American sister looked at the precious handkerchief and decided to share it. She cut it in half, framed each half and sent one to her younger "sister" in Japan with the note, "Our tears are mingled in this cloth. It was too precious to launder it."

Sometimes, participants discovered that their grandfathers, fathers, or uncles fought on opposing sides during World War II. As they embraced each other, they felt the soothing energy of healing and forgiveness, forever changing their perspectives. Many shared their stories.

Over the next few years, we held Bridge of Peace Ceremonies throughout America. The bridge gained spiritual power all its own as it became a source for reconciliation and healing energy among women representing racial, national, generational, and religious differences. Whatever her background, and whatever her difference, each woman crossed the bridge to embrace her sister in a reconciled relationship of love and forgiveness. Throughout America, Bridge of Peace ceremonies made a statement for peace and unity in many cities. Many celebrities were invited to entertain.

Actress Shirley Jones crosses the bridge in Los Angeles.

*John Denver not only provided entertainment from the stage,
he did group sing-alongs with the audience, pleasing everyone
with his popular songs.*

Worldwide, WFWP held ceremonies in places like Israel, where we reached out to Palestinian and Israeli women. Women in other nations sought reconciliation with each other as well. I know Mother Moon still longs for the day when women in North and South Korea will cross the bridge to eliminate the ideological barrier that divides them.

Through the leadership of our Founders, I had the opportunity to serve the cause of world peace. The Bridge of Peace reconciliation ceremony holds a special place in my heart. For seven years, I was the president of the Women's Federation for World Peace in America and the international vice president. I am proud of the wonderful women who still help bring *the logic of love* to our world. *Logic of love* is a term used by Mother Moon in some of her speeches.

CHAPTER 13

Planting Seeds:
China and North Korea

For the foreseeable future, it may be difficult to establish WFWP chapters and activities in China and North Korea or to reach these nations with the ideals of healing, forgiveness, and peace.

The unification of North and South Korea is something many Korean hearts long for, on both sides of the border, but there must be complex negotiations, difficult concessions, and greater trust before many steps can be taken toward unity. China is an economic, political, and military power whose influence no other country can ignore. Both nations embrace communism as their official ideology, and both are unlikely to tolerate expression of dissent or independent thought from their citizenry.

I believe God sees the world with the eyes of a loving parent who will open doors and hearts whenever and wherever possible. Spiritual victories don't always happen with fanfare. Forgiveness and reconciliation can happen gradually, in small symbolic ways or on an internal level. The journey of a thousand miles begins with a single step, and sometimes, all we must do is show up.

Beijing—World Conference on Women

In August 1995, Beijing, China, was the designated location for the United Nations Fourth World Conference on Women. Hillary Clinton spoke, and women attended from all over the world. At the same time, in the Beijing suburb of Huairou, nongovernment organizations, or NGOs, were given an opportunity to organize events for grassroots women's groups from many nations to share their situations and concerns. As an NGO, the WFWP scheduled an event in Huairou and arranged for Maureen Reagan, daughter of President Ronald Reagan, to give a keynote address on family values. Ms. Reagan had become a good friend through the Bridge of Peace ceremonies.

Arranging this event was no small job. For example, our packet of registration papers for the conference arrived just one day before we were scheduled to leave for China. I had arranged for Ms. Reagan, who asked to be called Maureen, to stay in one of three hotels in Huairou. Our WFWP members were registered in new but hastily built apartments, which would later serve as housing for Chinese citizens.

Welcome to the Hotel!

Maureen, Shirley (another American member), and I arrived in China after dark. At the airport in Beijing, we boarded a van that was transporting people to Huairou. Riding with us was a group of Baha'i faith members from America. It was raining, and we were dropped off with our luggage at a muddy stop along the road. Unblinking Chinese soldiers stood guard as we trooped through the mud with other women from all over the world, pulling or carrying our luggage. It was pure chaos!

We found a humble registration building where we were directed to our living quarters. Still carrying our suitcases, we walked to our lodgings in the dark. Maureen's hotel reservation did not seem to exist, so she went with us to our apartment complex. We carried our luggage up narrow stairs to the third floor, where we found our assigned rooms.

We opened the door to our luxurious hotel suite! The walls were white-washed cement that left white marks on our clothes if we brushed against them. Each single bed had a thin mattress, a sheet, and a pillow. Strung across the ceiling in each of our rooms was a wire from which one glaring light bulb hung. There was a small table, a lamp, and a chair. Each three-bedroom apartment had one small shower closet with a simple faucet.

After settling in, we went in search of the designated place to eat, a large cafeteria with plenty of food. There, we filled our trays and found seats beside a group of women from Canada. One lady did not have a tray, and Maureen offered to share her own, since there was more than enough food on it. I watched as the lady looked at Maureen's name tag and said, "Are you *the* Maureen Reagan?" Maureen laughed and nodded, "Yes." It was such a paradox. Here was a president's daughter sharing her food in a humble cafeteria in China with a Canadian woman whom she did not know. That was Maureen!

Whenever I apologized for our uncomfortable conditions, Maureen said it was an adventure for her, one she could talk about in the future. She enjoyed mixing with a variety of people, and she laughed easily.

The next day, with help from the staff of the American Embassy, we found a small suite in the hotel for Maureen. She immediately set up shop for us to make her suite a headquarters where we would meet every morning and gather again at mealtimes. Shirley took on the mission of caring for Maureen, to make certain that Maureen had everything she needed and even gave her Reiki treatments!

Claiming a Venue

When the day came for Maureen's speech, it was scorching hot. We had posted fliers that read, "Celebrate the Family: Hear Maureen Reagan

Speak." Our contingent of WFWP members from South Korea, Japan, and other nations were distributing flyers to publicize the event. When we went to set up our meeting in our assigned building, another group was setting up in our space! We were told that rooms were available on a first-come, first-served basis, and if we could find another space, we could use it.

I am introducing Maureen Reagan. She is holding a fan since
it was a very hot day and the large room was not air conditioned.

Off we went in search of a venue for our program. We found a large unoccupied room that seated about 400 people, and we claimed it! We had a banner to hang, but no work force, no hammer, no nails, and no ladder. We did our best, but photos will attest to the fact that amateurs had secured our banner, and it was hanging precariously. We made a line of WFWP women, including Japanese, Korean, and other international women to direct people from our advertised site to our new location. To our delight, the room filled up quickly, with about 500 women in attendance. Initially, there was no microphone, but Maureen was a trooper, and she won everyone's heart as she spoke on the renaissance of the family. At one point, she said, "No one can value the family if they hold no value for the women in it." The audience loved her message, and we considered her speech a success, despite all the disconnects that we had experienced.

There were other problems. The pamphlets produced for the event never reached us. Betty, a friend of WFWP from Washington, had brought a whole carton with her, but she couldn't find us. We didn't have cell phones, and there was no central communications system, so we resorted to leaving messages for her at various places. In the end, she brought the pamphlets back to America. I will never forget the crestfallen look on the face of Mrs. Lan Young Moon, the international president of WFWP, when she discovered the pamphlets were not available.

Betsy Jones, vice president of WFWP-USA, had traveled separately from my group. Upon her arrival, the registration desk directed her to the wrong housing arrangements and it took several days for her to find us. As a resourceful person, she spent time in a valuable way, interacting with women from many nations who had come to attend the conference, but she was feeling anxious until she connected with us.

I will end this story on a sweet note: Around midnight each night, after the others in my group had turned in, I went outside to a staging area where a large group of women from Africa gathered to dance and sing. Dressed in gorgeously colored dresses and headdresses, they danced to their own music into the wee hours of the morning. Watching them lifted my heart. Their clothes were a feast for my eyes, their music a feast for my ears, and their movements a feast for my soul. During the day, they shared the suffering of the women of their nations, but at night, they laid aside their troubles and let their spirits soar.

Outreach to North Korea

We were going to North Korea, the hermit nation. For over fifty years, few outsiders had set foot on its soil and people had suffered for years under oppressive leadership. Most ordinary citizens had experienced deprivation of adequate food, housing, and hope. The WFWP international office in South Korea was able to arrange for 700 women to travel to North Korea for an exchange of greetings and speeches.

Hyundai Asan owned a resort across the border and ran a tourist business for South Koreans to go on tours of the Kumgangsan Mountain area in North Korea. We traveled on this mission as a part of a tourist group.

My Journal Entries:

It took over three hours to drive to the Gosong area on buses. There, we went through the South Korea checkpoint with our luggage, then boarded other buses. We drove through the demilitarized zone and entered the North Korean checkpoint. The contrast in checkpoints was incredible. Whereas the southern checkpoint was very modern, new and clean, the northern checkpoint was a building made of canvas tied to a framework of metal poles. Propaganda music greeted us. The staff was stoic, but civil.

After boarding the buses, we rode through North Korea to our mountain destination. It was a single road with a light green metal fence on each side that separated us from the very barren countryside. Small ridges between the fields separated patches of soil. An occasional lone figure was walking or working in the field; sometimes several people were working together. On some occasions, we saw a person pushing a wooden plow behind an animal. Twice we saw a tractor-type vehicle—never a car—and a few trucks. Once we saw a bus parked along a gravel road with many people walking across the fields toward it.

Occasionally, there was an enclave of small houses. All were white, one-story dwellings. All were very simple, looked old, and had tile roofs. There were several little villages with schoolyards and children playing outside. Once we saw children marching. The only larger buildings were very old and looked like school buildings. Another place looked like military housing with very, very small, newer looking houses. The ground was barren. Some creeks or rivers were nearly dry. Maybe they filled up with the spring thaw from the mountains. It was very rocky, with many large smooth, round rocks. There were some patches of fresh-looking green plants, maybe chicory or mustard greens.

All along the way, solitary soldiers stood guard. They were thin and stoic; there was no movement, or any expression on their faces. "Was there any joy in life?" I wondered. We were busloads of laughing, chatting women. We had homes, families, and food to return to. Did they have anything? Life looked so bleak.

After driving through this bleak countryside, we came upon a modern, glitzy plaza with a number of buildings including five or six stores and five or six restaurants. There was a large convention center where entertainment took place and meetings were held. Driving further up the hill, we saw three large, modern hotels where our busloads of women were dropped.

My good friend, Betsy, and I were given a room on the 11th floor. After all the travel, this was a welcoming and comfortable place. The hotel was furnished beautifully with chandeliers, and central stairs. The rooms on some of the floors had platform beds, while others had mats on the floor. The whole complex of hotels was a tourist area completely separated from the North Korean countryside and created for the South Korean tourist trade centered on the beautiful mountain and beach areas offered by nature. We were given tickets to use in the restaurants of our choice. Shops offered typical tourist ware: i.e., jewelry, t-shirts, sweatshirts, and all kinds of souvenirs. Everything was overpriced.

In addition to our group of 700 women, many tourist groups from

South Korea had come to climb the mountain. We were unique in that we were mostly international women. In contrast to the glitzy tourist plaza that was established and run as a business, the mountains were a thing of untainted natural beauty. The autumn leaves were still intact. We climbed a rather wide upward slope that was paved in concrete where designs were laid with stones—geometric shapes and flower shapes with edgings and strips. Larger rocks formed the edges. Occasionally there was a stone bench. At other places, there was a large rock with carved writings in red. These were said to be revered and held sacred—and not to be touched. Also high in the mountains one could see words carved into the rocks. These were said to be writings of Mao Zedong.

The views were stunning: Mountains of rock formations, jagged and vertical, reached skyward like giant fingers reaching for the sun. At other places, the rocks were smooth and worn. Everywhere hills and mountains created grand vistas that were breathtaking. We could climb at our own pace and turn around before reaching the top if we wanted. The path was crowded with thousands of South Koreans from other tours. They were obviously comfortable with mountain climbing and headed energetically for the goal. With their hiking gear and walking sticks, many older people left us in the dust as they climbed the slopes. At some places, there were steps.

All was pristine nature and obviously an attempt was made to keep it pure and free of litter. We were instructed that no rocks, leaves or any other items were to be taken with us. In fact, there would be enormous fines at the border if we were found to have them in our possession. Only rocks bought in the shops were accepted at the checkpoint.

At the Convention Center in North Korea, the WFWP program began with an opening session on the first evening. We had been riding on the bus all day and everyone was quite tired. However, we donned our 700 purple WFWP tee-shirts and went to the culture center where Mrs. Lan Young Moon and other WFWP leaders gave short presentations. A somewhat subtle but not-so-subtle slideshow presented Mother Moon and her children in the context of parenthood. A North Korean woman designee read a speech. We could tell it was carefully crafted and delivered formally, without emotion. The speaker mentioned Kim Il Sung and talked about the beauty of the mountain. There were six ladies from North Korea; all dressed up in beautiful Korean chima chogories. There was little opportunity for give-and-take with them. They were definitely handpicked and dressed up as North Korean representatives to our WFWP event.

The following evening, we had a closing meeting in the same place. We all received a candle. After a short program, we lit each other's candles, turned out the lights and sang Tongil, which is a Korean song of unity.

Our mission was a serious one—to make a connection with North Korea. The tourist trappings were almost painful when we thought of the needs of the North Korean people. At least, we made the beginnings of a relationship between women from both Koreas. WFWP in Korea began a program called 1% through which South Korean women could give 1% of their income to assist their northern neighbors. I returned to America with a grateful heart for our freedom and a sad heart for the oppressed peoples of North Korea.

The One That Did Not Get Away

We had just finished a meeting at East Garden, the Moon's residence in New York, when Father announced he was going fishing on the Hudson River. He invited the WFWP leaders to go with him, and I was guided to be on Father Moon's boat. Seldom in my life had I gone fishing, and I was not comfortable getting on the boat with a bunch of Korean anglers. They kindly helped me to set up my rod and reel, and I cast out my line.

Father Moon set up his operation in the bow of the boat, and I sat in the stern to wait for a bite. As I waited, I thought, "Father puts much significance into catching fish. As the president of WFWP in America, I do not want to disappoint him by not catching anything. I must catch a fish for the sake of WFWP!"

Suddenly I felt a tug on my line! It was difficult to reel the fish in, and some of the men helped. Hearing the commotion behind him, Father Moon turned around and asked, "Who caught it?" Besides the fish he caught a little later, it was the biggest catch of the day—a thirty-two-inch striped bass!

Three WFWP leaders fishing in Alaska; myself, Josette and Betsy

Connection Awareness

Once I became determined to make a "good catch," I got results. From this experience, I learned there was a connection between my thoughts and catching a fish. This made me more aware of the connection between my thoughts and all of nature, my thoughts and all the events of my life! Everything is more connected than we realize.

I could look at the external outcomes of our WFWP efforts in China and North Korea and wonder about their impact. We might think that those efforts did not amount to much, but we had done everything we could. We had backed up our sincere motivation with our presence and with the output of our physical and spiritual energy. The fishing expedition had taught me to expect a positive result.

I concluded that how I thought about events mattered. I would claim our efforts in communist China and North Korea as successes on every level. I recalled how the Eastern clerics in the spirit world had come through a medium to thank me for our prayers for Lithuania. Maybe we had made a bigger impact in the heavens than we had on earth. I just needed to gain greater awareness of how the ripple effects of our words, actions, and efforts can extend beyond what we can see in this dimension.

CHAPTER 14

Writing It Down

My work with WFWP was all about peace in the world. I also wanted to maintain peace within myself. For me, one way to do this is to write. Since childhood, writing has been my passion. Putting my thoughts down on paper makes me feel connected to my inner being on a higher plane. I think best with a pen in hand, and I love to feel the flow of writing in longhand. Journaling has given me a way to internalize experiences, thoughts, feelings, and inspirations. Writing has also been a way to share with others. During my years of serving as director of the Blessed Family Department, I edited the *Blessing Quarterly* and later the *Blessed Family Journal.* It was my joy to write about an inspiration or a lesson learned. On several occasions, I put together my inspirations and published them.

A Publication

In 1994, the death of Linna, a friend and colleague, inspired me to write a booklet that focused on life after death. It was titled *Insights into the Afterlife.*

From the Introduction:

Linna and I were friends and colleagues. She was an educator and a woman of determination. It was a shock to all her friends when she was diagnosed with cancer. I remember visiting her in the hospital where she joked, "We always thought I was the invincible one, so we have life insurance on my husband!"

Following surgery and chemotherapy, Linna began a new life. It was a life with greater awareness of its value. She looked at her relationships with family and friends with new eyes. She pondered the things she wanted to accomplish and those things that were of less importance. She sought changes in her life and habits to bring about optimum health. She began meditating and, in so doing, found a place of peace within, as well as a greater spiritual awareness. She made changes in her diet and found friends who prayed for her and introduced her to healing music, writings on positive thinking, healing imagery, and internal body cleansing.

Her friends saw her blossom and make gains in spiritual and physical health. However, underlying everything was a nagging fear that the cancer would snatch away her life. And so, it did. She had four and one-half years to accomplish things she wanted to do, time to prepare with her husband and grown children, and most of all, time to think about life after death. In the final six months, Linna knew that her life on earth was ending. Her concern was, "What should I accomplish, and how can I best prepare to die?" During this time, a close group of her friends learned much about death—and life thereafter.

My heart aches for the many who die without preparation, without a sustaining philosophy of life, or death. This is the primary reason that I asked a few close friends of Linna to help me in preparing this little booklet to share what we have learned through our experience with her, and through our own reading and searching. If there is life after death and if our earthly life is preparation for that, then we have come to believe the greatest thing we could do for humankind is to share this understanding.

For the format of this informative booklet, I chose 30 commonly asked questions with answers that the reader would find simple and clear. These answers are presented without specific religious doctrine and are for the sole purpose of enhancing life both on earth and in the beyond. This booklet is for those who are in the full bloom of life—for there is still time to prepare. For those who are terminally ill, it might make a difference in the quality of the final years or months and help the new arrival into the spiritual world. For those who have had a loved one pass on, it may be a comfort to know that life continues.

Answers to the thirty questions in the booklet were gleaned from testimonies of near-death experiences and other writings as well as ideas and submissions from some of Linna's close friends. The booklet was published by our church under its official name, the Holy Spirit Association for the Unification of World Christianity. Since its initial publication, it has been translated into four languages.

Father Moon autographed my book, **Insights into the Afterlife.**

Linna was also a writer. She had composed short stories for children that were published regularly in the *Blessed Family Journal*. After she passed away, these stories became a book for children called *Light of Glory: Children's Stories on the Early Days of the Unification Church*.

Circles of Angels

In 1995, while serving as the American president of WFWP, I wrote *Circles of Angels*, a small book describing some of the experiences I had when I called on angels to help me in my work:

From the Introduction:

It began when I was sitting in my office looking at stacks of papers, each representing a project, a group of people, or an undeveloped idea. I felt overwhelmed, wondering how I could bring each of these tasks and projects to completion. I pondered: How could I delegate some of this work? To whom could I give these projects? I needed God's perspective. I asked how I might engage spiritual help.

Working through the stacks, I found myself humming a piece of a song I remembered from childhood:

"Oh come, Angel band!

Come and around me stand."

An angel band! What an interesting concept. I envisioned a band of angels surrounding me, ready to help. Yes, that was it. I would call on them for help. Was there not some understanding that angel help was only a prayer away? My sense of feeling overwhelmed vanished as the angel band idea took shape. I kept envisioning a circle of heavenly beings dancing around me. They were comforting and peaceful and created a warm feeling. They were also energetic and vibrant. They were a special band of angels, united in heart and creating spiritual energy for healing, protection, and inspiration. I could sense the stirring of the air as they whirled around me.

When I browsed through new releases in bookstores, I was fascinated with the current interest in angels. It seems that we are finally becoming aware of spiritual help, which has always been available! Is God, who is infinite love, sending greater angelic energy to earth, moving us toward a more spiritual age?

Although I have always believed in angels, I began to feel excitement about the possibility of greater spiritual energy waiting to be released. If such power is available, perhaps I could tap into it—for example, visualizing bands of angels around those I pray for may make my prayers more expansive, more comprehensive, and more powerful.

According to most definitions, angels are God's special servants, created to protect, guide, guard, heal, and comfort us and act as messengers. Angels are believed to be practically innumerable. The Bible refers to their being called by the tens of thousands, and that myriads of heavenly hosts are being "poured out" upon the earth. If they are awaiting a commission, how can I summon them? Thus began an exciting personal journey into a realm of learning how to engage spiritual help and companionship.

God had given me an answer to my call for help and, after using this help, I decided to share it in the form of a small book. Some of my friends also encouraged me to share my experiences with creating a "band" or "circle" of angels as my extended staff.

Since writing this book, I have called on groups of angels to help me in all kinds of circumstances. I do not see them, but I can feel that they pave the way for life to flow more easily. I have consistently assigned angels to missions and given them job descriptions and specific instructions, asking them to bring angelic energy into every situation. What brings me the greatest joy is the knowledge that groups of angels are helping people all over the world. Recently I received an email from a man whom I did not know in Poland asking for permission to translate the book into the Polish language and publish it. He said he wanted this to become a way to help his country. He did publish it, and I am so happy he could help spread the word.

Our Business is Their Business

Several years ago, my husband and I were working with a realtor to sell a church-owned property. In speaking with a wealthy entrepreneur who was looking at the property, we discovered that he wanted to create a spiritual and educational center for young people. I felt inspired to give him a copy of *Circles of Angels.* He loved the concept of calling on angels for help. A week later, he showed me his office, and on his desk was a framed quote from my book. It was a copy of a prayer I have used to summon angels.

One never knows how far the written word will travel. For over twenty years and after three reprints, the book has been purchased by many people, most recently on Amazon, and I often give speeches on the topic. One of my favorite places to speak on angels is in senior centers.

Lorna Byrne, an Irish writer, sees angels everywhere and writes about her observations. About four years ago, I attended a speech she was giving in Boston. One thing she said resonated with my own angel work. "There are three kinds of angels," she said. "Guardian angels are given to everyone in the world and stay with them always." Then she explained about angels with a mission who are assigned to help people, projects, healing, and even nations. "The third kind of angels," she said, "are the unemployed angels.

They are awaiting assignments and are happy to help if we ask them to do so." These words rang true to me.

Signing copies of Circle of Angels in a bookstore.

Mary's Story

Mary, a friend from my quilters' club, shared the following amazing story with members of our group:

After reading an article on my work in the *Clermont Neighbors Magazine,* she decided to buy a copy of *Circle of Angels.* The book arrived from Amazon just before she left to visit her daughter, and she took it with her to read on the plane. When she arrived, her daughter tearfully told her that her one-year-old son had just been found to have a mass on his head. The CT scan and all the tests showed he would need surgery immediately.

Shocked by the news, Mary thought of *Circles of Angels* and felt that God had placed it in her hands at this time of need. She shared it with her daughter, and they prayed for a circle of angels to surround her grandson and guide the surgery. They also asked members of her church to send angels to help.

The surgery was scheduled for the following day. The one-year-old boy had his head shaved and was fully prepped. As the surgical team wheeled him into the operating room, the family continued to pray. A short time later, the surgeon returned and reported, "I will not be operating. I don't have an explanation for this, but there is no detectible mass. After a thorough examination and more tests, I can find nothing there to remove." Mary, her family, and their church congregation rejoiced. "This is a miracle," they agreed. They thanked God and the angels for intervening. With a face glowing in gratitude, Mary shared this beautiful story with our quilters' group.

It isn't always easy to share one's views about spiritual topics with new friends, but I made the decision in graduate school, years ago, not to hide who I am from people. That decision has served me well and sometimes helped others. By sharing this little book in my local community, I am promoting a universally available source of help and healing—circles of angels—and deepened relationships in my circles of friends.

Value of Writing

I sometimes have fleeting inspirations that come and go without sticking power. If I write them down, I am more likely to flesh them out and act on them. Writing always helps me plan projects and make decisions.

Keeping a journal is like having a friend. I can record important life events, clarify my thoughts, process challenging emotions, or see in greater detail the view outside my window. Writing on a quote that captures my imagination provides a creative outlet and enhances my understanding of what I like about these particular words.

I sometimes get more inspiration while writing, and when that happens, my thinking expands. Writing this memoir has helped me to better see the connections between events and people who have influenced me. It has helped me understand myself better in relation to God and those I love the most.

CHAPTER 15

New Horizons

We were living in McLean, Virginia, while I continued to serve as president of Women's Federation in America, and Hugh was working on the staff of the *Washington Golf Monthly*.

In August 1996, Hugh and I joined other couples in a forty-day workshop in Cheongpyeong, Korea. The Church was making an effort to enlist American couples to support the providential work of Unification churches worldwide. At the end of the workshop, through a unique lottery process, we received the country of Nicaragua as our nation to serve.

When we visited Nicaragua in order to determine how we could help, we saw extreme poverty and soon realized the mission there would be better served if we supported projects from the United States where we had more resources. We identified two important needs: education and technology. We saw how important it was for the youth of Nicaragua to have a genuine chance to improve their economic status. If they gained greater knowledge and skills, we also believed it would change the future of the country. We returned to America to explore ways to educate youth in Nicaragua through a distance learning educational program.

Nicaragua was still recovering from a devastating earthquake some 20 years before our visit.

A New Residential High School

With this in mind, we visited the University of Bridgeport in Connecticut in December 1996, seeking input and potential resources. Soon after that visit, Hugh was asked to start a boarding high school for second-generation church members using an unoccupied dormitory on the university campus. Hugh stepped down from his position at the magazine. In accepting this mission as the headmaster of a school, we hoped we could find a way to address some of the needs of Nicaraguan youth as well. Based on research that had already been done, Hugh began planning for the school. Initially, Hugh spent weekdays in Bridgeport, and our family continued living in McLean, Virginia, but in June 1997, we moved to Bridgeport. My seven-year term as president of WFWP in America ended, and a capable replacement, Alexa, was appointed.

I have a master's degree in social work. Hugh has a doctorate in American history. My work in the Blessed Family Department, the American and international mission field, and the Womens Federation for World Peace, gave me a skill set that I knew could be useful. Hugh had many management skills and experiences as a church leader and non-profit administrator. He is a scholar in his field. We thought we knew what to expect in terms of the kind of missions we might be called on to lead or support, but this new assignment was a complete surprise to us!

When offered the job, I didn't feel prepared. We were being asked to develop and operate a private residential high school for children of church members, a challenging task even for experienced professional educators. We had no credentials or experience specific to the job, but we gradually realized we had extensive knowledge, skills, and abilities that would help us fulfill this mission.

We had advanced degrees and years of experience in administration of non-profit organizations. We had developed and managed many different facilities, taught the Divine Principle, and taught others how to teach it. We had supervised many staff members and led groups of young people in centers and on traveling teams, taking responsibility for their security and well-being. We knew how to learn. Most of all, we were fully committed to the church and to this mission.

We had been trusted by our Founders with development of an accredited, college preparatory school that would offer an excellent academic program, a healthy social environment, and a culture that reflected the values of our religious movement. It was service that would affect many young lives, and we prayerfully took it to heart.

Husband and Wife Educators

In September, New Eden Academy became a reality with seventy students enrolled in the inaugural class. Hugh was the headmaster. The next year I became the vice principal of the school. Having traveled extensively as an IW and with WFWP, I was ready to settle down, work with my husband, and be much more available to our grown children. The youngest, High, who was still at home, was a student at the University of Bridgeport.

My earlier missions were broad and expansive, requiring me to travel all over the U.S. and the world, often staying only a brief time in one place. It would be different indeed to plant myself at the new high school and let the roots grow deep. I could make lasting relationships, help build an institution, and leave a legacy for future generations. I was excited.

I took on the teaching of character education, art, writing, and public speaking. Educating youth meant investing in the future, and leading a school and teaching meant I could put my creative juices to work. On a deeper level, this new mission meant that I could be a channel for God's energy to flow, and I felt that it did. It was also an opportunity to enlist angelic help. I summoned a circle of angels to surround every student, and I would continue doing that at the beginning of each year. I did the same thing for teachers, staff, and administrators, embracing everyone with the protective energy brought by God's heavenly messengers.

Problem-Solving

It was not easy to start a residential high school or to establish and maintain the high academic and ethical standards that we had in mind. In developing the school, Hugh had been through many legal and administrative hurdles, including obtaining state approval and eventually regional accreditation. We were told that ours was the first new boarding school established in Connecticut in many decades.

When Hugh filed for approval from the Connecticut State Department of Health to have an infirmary for a boarding school, he hit a legal barrier. There were extensive government regulations for an infirmary, including the requirement that there be a helipad, in case a student had to be airlifted to a hospital. Astonished by this news, Hugh commissioned an attorney who was also a nurse to help. She easily and quickly solved the problem by advising us to call our medical facility a health center instead of an infirmary, since it had fewer regulatory requirements.

A New Institution—a New Tradition

Initially, our academy was a high school for children of Unification Church families, i.e., second-generation teenagers who came to the school to live and study. It was hard to deny admission to students who were unwilling or unable to meet the academic and behavioral standards we set. In those early years, we had to deal with drug use by several students in the first two classes. In one situation, when driving around at lunchtime, I found students hiding in a park. I picked them up, searched their bags, and found drugs.

Local educators recognized our academic program as excellent. The school was also known for its drama, digital arts, and character education programs. I strongly believed in educating youth to speak and write well, knowing that those skills were every bit as valuable as academic knowledge.

With good up-front communications and vigilance once we admitted students, we conquered drug use at the school. Slowly, our student body evolved to become a group of sincere youth who wanted to learn and grow. When I see some of the young leaders in our church today, I thank God that we were part of their education and development.

New Eden Academy opened in Cooper Hall, which was a dormitory on the campus of the University of Bridgeport. After three years, the executive committee of the UB Board of Trustees decided that a church school should not be located on a private, nonsectarian university campus.

The decision by the university became a catalyst for change. In consultation with Rev. Moon, the school was renamed Bridgeport International

Academy, aka BIA. We adopted new articles of incorporation with a broader, nonsectarian mission—to educate international youth of all religions, races, and ethnic backgrounds. Students were admitted and retained based on their willingness to uphold the specific principles and standards of the school. Excellent fine arts and theater programs became a popular attraction in addition to the high-quality academic curriculum.

We opened our doors to students who were not members of the Unification Church. With those start-up legal and financial issues behind us, we were ready to move forward and find a new building.

Hugh poses with some of the actors after a production of Shakespeare's A Midsummer Night's Dream.

Becoming a High School Principal

On March 25, 2005, Hugh and I were at the breakfast table at East Garden. Suddenly Father Moon asked me to take on the role of the principal of BIA, then asked Betsy Jones and Marie Ang to form a support trinity with me. He said he was calling on us as "the mothers of the American church" to work together to nurture, educate, and lead the next generation, thus preparing them to become future leaders. We were to educate not only American students. His vision for the Academy was to be a truly international school whose graduates would become leaders who had experienced a mini-global community. Two days later on Easter Sunday, we were again at East Garden. Betsy, Marie, and I were standing together when I suddenly heard my name called by Father Moon: "I'm going to provide a grant of two million dollars to BIA either to buy or to construct a school building."

Hugh delivers the commencement address to a BIA graduating class.

All heads turned toward me in surprise. I felt great gratitude for the grant but also a keen sense of increased responsibility. Again, I reflected on my lack of specific training, experience, or credentials to serve as a professional educator. This made me hesitant to become the principal of the school, but it was happening! I was confident that I could bring a flow of spiritual energy and protection for the students, I knew I could learn what

I needed to know, and I knew I would not have to do it alone. Hugh would still be there, we had a capable staff, and I could trust God and the angels to lend a hand whenever I asked for it.

Marie, Betsy, and I received the surprise announcement of a large donation to BIA.

I had my training as a social worker, my years as an administrative leader, and my experience in supervising the work of others and delegating responsibilities. I knew I was good at problem-solving, and I had the help of the angels! What could go wrong?

As president of our senior high school, Hugh continued to focus on the legal, fiscal, enrollment, facility and management issues. He taught history courses. I focused on the academic program and human resources, especially the well-being of the faculty, staff and students. Betsy brought her skills as a nurse to our health center. She traveled from Albany, New York, several days each week to serve in this role. Traveling from New Jersey, Marie brought her expertise as a teacher to create a system for evaluating our faculty and students. Betsy, Marie, and their husbands also served for many years on the Board of Trustees of Bridgeport International Academy.

Bridgeport International Academy

A New Location

Having received a large grant from the church, we set about finding a suitable facility for our school. After an extensive search, we decided to renovate the Seaside Institute building that was owned by BIA and was adjacent to the university campus. In 1886, Seaside Institute was established as a boarding school for teenage girls and was dedicated by Frances Folsom Cleveland, the wife of President Grover Cleveland. Later the building was expanded and converted into thirty apartments. We renovated the second floor of the stately, three-story building to house beautiful, modern classrooms, offices, an assembly room, and a multi-purpose room, which was named Spurgin

Hall after we retired from leadership of the school.

The plaque for Spurgin Hall

Visits from Irene and Sandy—Two Hurricanes

The new location of Bridgeport International Academy was within view of the beautiful Seaside Park on the Long Island Sound. We enjoyed this location and gave no consideration to the possibility of flooding that would result from hurricanes, since that was not a common occurrence in

Connecticut. Then, on August 28, 2011 all that changed when a visit from Hurricane Irene brought damaging water from the ocean into the first floor of the building. The elementary school and apartments on that lower level of the building were severely damaged resulting in major repairs. It was a financial blow from which we were able to recover by obtaining a Small Business Administration loan. Many local church members helped with the renovations, and we were able to continue our classes.

Then, one year later on October 29, we had another visit! This time from Hurricane Sandy, which devastated much of the northeastern coastline. I was visiting my friend, Anne, in Phoenix, Arizona at that time. Hugh called to inform me that the school and the apartments, including our apartment, had been flooded and that the first floor was under 16 inches of water. With the help of BIA students and staff, he had managed to salvage much of our personal belongings and furniture.

Hugh said, "From the second floor I watched a sea wall of ocean water come rushing down the street toward our building, but there was nothing I could do to stop it." After the previous hurricane, the Federal Emergency Management Agency had designated our building to be within the flood zone, requiring that we obtain flood insurance, which we did six weeks before the second hurricane hit. That was certainly a blessing. FEMA estimated the damage to our school building to be $ 1.1 million, and we again set about addressing the devastation.

An Accreditation Visit

After eight years of operation with approval solely from the state of Connecticut, we applied for accreditation with the New England Association of Schools and Colleges. Our capable faculty, staff, students and parents pulled together to write a self-study, making sure that everything was in top shape. Betsy took part in an accreditation visit at another school and brought that experience back to us. She helped with plans for the visit of the professional educators.

Hosting an accreditation visit by a team of seven professional educators requires no small amount of preparation. The accreditation team would evaluate every aspect of the operation of our school and make recommendations to the New England Association of Schools and Colleges. For three days in 2006, we welcomed the visiting team openly. Faculty, students, and parents were available to them to share information about our school.

On the second day of the visit, a faculty member took me aside and said, "Nora I have had the same dream two nights in a row. In the dream, I was given a pair of three-dimensional glasses and told to wear them. When I put them on, I could see angels filling the corridors of the school. As the visiting team entered and walked down the main corridor, angels were greeting them along the way. There was a welcoming atmosphere. I think this dream was meant to be shared with you."

The message was that angels were helping our school and wanted to make their presence known to us! I had summoned them with faith that they would bring energy to the project I had asked them to support. Later, we received a letter confirming that we had received accreditation with New England's most prestigious accrediting agency. I have no doubt that the angels helped the accreditation visit to go well.

Expansion

Over several years, the school continued to expand its enrollment. Brian, a parent and a BIA trustee, helped us to recruit international students. We broadened our curriculum to include classes in English as a Second Language, and we reached out initially to Japanese, Korean, and Chinese students. Later, we invited students from many other countries to apply as well.

Between February 2010 and January 2013, Brian arranged for three recruitment trips to China. I visited schools and recruitment fairs in eight cities in China, and Hugh represented our school at fairs in Shanghai and Taipei, Taiwan. It was an opportunity for us to meet recruiters from other schools and learn much about educating foreign students. The inclusion of international students generated much-needed revenue, and the increased diversity in the student body helped the school flourish.

The students and faculty of Bridgeport International Academy

A Staff that Multi-tasks

As in any small school, we needed teachers and staff who were willing to take on multiple roles. I was the principal, but I also had other roles. As academic guidance counselor, I found joy in aiding the graduates to choose colleges and universities that were a good fit for them. The students were bright, talented, fine young people, and writing recommendations that accurately reflected their accomplishments required careful thought. My desire was to see each of them find the college that would meet their academic and social needs and prepare them to contribute to our society. I wanted them to find happiness and fulfillment in career, community, and family life.

I enjoyed giving speeches and viewed giving the commencement address as my well-crafted farewell gift to our students. For my last commencement speech, I chose to write a story set forty years in the future that included each of the eighteen graduates. I watched the anticipation on their faces as they awaited their names in the story. Delivering that speech was a lot of fun!

I also served as the school's yearbook advisor. Producing the 2005-06 yearbook was an unforgettable experience. On the evening before the deadline to submit the publication, four of the most diligent team members were doing a final read-through. Suddenly I heard a gasp! Next, I heard, "Mrs. Spurgin! We accidentally deleted the whole book!" Frantically, they sought to recover the yearbook, but to no avail. We looked at each other in horror. "What can we do now?" one of them asked, as panic set in.

I said, "Can you pull an all-nighter?" Those four bright, hard-working students shook their heads affirmatively. Working together through the night, we assembled the original materials and used them to create a new book. When the morning dawned, we had done the job! We all went to Dunkin Donuts and celebrated with breakfast. They were my heroes, and I will never forget them.

When I retired as principal of Bridgeport International Academy in July 2016, I wrote the following thoughts in a letter to parents:

During these nineteen years, Bridgeport International Academy moved from its original home in Cooper Hall on the campus of the University of Bridgeport to its current location on Lafayette Street. I remember with nostalgia how the renovation of the current school building drew upon my passion for beauty and design. As I leave my role as its principal, I reflect on this in the many choices that were made. Whether it was in the school's colors, the placement of rooms and furniture in the designs and plans of courses and activities, or with the faculty and staff hired—or most importantly, to me —in the modeling of integrity, honor and warmth, I am satisfied with knowing that a job was well done and a foundation of education secured at this school for future generations of BIA students.

I have always believed that a well-educated person should be able to write and speak well, and it was my passion to teach the students these attributes. I have also believed that a successful person is educated in the mind and in the heart. As I leave our school and observe this years upcoming graduation I feel so proud of each student whose life has been touched at BIA, knowing that the world will be a better place because of them. I am happy that I have had a small part in helping to shape their lives.

Lastly, I am grateful for the opportunity to have served at BIA.

Farewell to our Beloved Founder

In September 2012 at 92 years of age, Reverend Sun Myung Moon passed on to his eternal home. As a devout Christian, at the age of fifteen, he received a spiritual visitation from Jesus while he was praying on a Korean mountainside one Easter morning. Jesus asked him to complete the mission of building the kingdom of God, saying that God had chosen him to fulfill this mission and had prepared the world for the coming of the kingdom of heaven on earth.

Reverend Moon lived every moment with purpose. He initiated innumerable organizations and projects worldwide to lead humankind into a world of peace where God could live among us in the kingdom of heaven on earth.

In the latter part of his life, Reverend Moon stated:

The world today is in a period when the participation of religious people is crucial. Those who have achieved deep self-awareness through religious practice are needed now more than ever. It is only truly religious people who can stand up to the unrighteousness and evil of the world and practice true love. It is only when the knowledge and experience of political leaders are combined with the wisdom of interreligious leaders that the world will be able to find the path to true peace.

Again today I set out on my path with renewed determination to achieve that goal. My prayer is that every person on earth will be reborn as a peace-loving global citizen, transcending barriers of religion, ideology, and race.

A man of God, the Reverend Moon lived a life of purpose, sacrifice, and love for humankind.

Under a communist regime in North Korea, Father Moon suffered greatly and was tortured. He was imprisoned for two years and eight months before being released by the American armed forces. Then he began his work anew in South Korea.

Unification Church members all over the world grieved the loss of their beloved leader and teacher. Father and Mother Moon had fourteen children. Several of them expected that they would succeed him, but his wife, Dr. Hak Ja Han Moon, assumed the mantle of leadership. Today, she brings the marriage blessing to large groups throughout the world to fulfill the central purpose of the church. In many third world countries, national leaders and large church groups have embraced her, inviting her to bring her message of peace and the marriage blessing to their people.

For many years, our Founders sought to achieve global interdependence, mutual prosperity and universal values. Through the Universal Peace Federation, Mother Moon has provided a forum for international religious and political leaders to promote these three principles as the foundation to realize peace worldwide.

After Reverend Moon passed away, Mrs. Moon traveled extensively worldwide holding summit meetings with major leaders. In America, she inspired large crowds through *Peace Starts with Me Rallies* in large cities. The division of her own homeland of Korea presents an ultimate challenge. She is passionate to end the suffering of her people and see them once again united and free. When the pandemic limited her travels, she continued her outreach through virtual *Rallies of Hope* where she and current and previous heads of state spoke about the need to unify the Korean peninsula.

For me, Father Moon clearly described his mission when he frequently said that he did not come to start a new church, but came to fulfill God's promise that all people will be brought together as one family under God. For this effort he and Mrs. Moon have labored tirelessly.

Now in her late seventies, Mother Moon is reaching out globally to political, religious and other leaders through the Universal Peace Federation, calling on them to unite in peace-making efforts. In her memoir, titled

Mother of Peace, she wrote:

> *Healthy societies of all races, nations and religions arise on the foundation of morality and ethics, which in turn arise on the foundation of the love of God between husband and wife, parents and children. This love of God in the family is the source of absolute values, values that are universally shared and taught by all religions.*

I like to visualize the work of kingdom building as a fountain. A small group of faithful members gather all their energy and strength to penetrate the cloud of darkness. Like a fountain, their efforts shoot upward with force and then return, creating a much larger pool of gentle droplets to nourish people on earth.

Another Mission for Hugh

In January 2015, the Unification Theological Seminary Board of Trustees chose Hugh to be its president. It was a demanding role, as he worked to satisfy requirements to reinstate the seminary's accreditation, manage its finances, move the primary campus to New York City, and set up an accredited, online program.

Frank LaGrotteria, a capable member of the Board of Trustees of Bridgeport International Academy, stepped into Hugh's role as president of BIA, and I continued as the principal, gradually relinquishing my responsibilities until I retired from my position in June 2016 at age 78.

I was ready to take care of pressing health issues, including hip and knee replacement surgeries, and take life at a slower pace. It was the beginning of a time of more "being" and less "doing." It was also an opportunity to help Hugh deal with the same financial challenges that many residential seminaries were facing in a fast-changing world. An increasing number of students were moving to online studies.

Maintaining the large, residential campus in Barrytown without boarding students was problematic. With pressure from church leaders to reduce the financial burden of that large property, a decision was made to sell it and consolidate UTS programs in New York City. Despite an exhaustive search, three offers were made, but none of them was financially acceptable to members of the UTS Board. They finally decided to keep the property as a venue for church events and youth activities.

While meeting with potential buyers, Hugh and I developed a relationship with the young entrepreneur who had a vision that he could use the property as a spiritual center for young adults. He shared that he felt he was guided by God to find a place to provide educational seminars for young people, and he thought the Barrytown property had a good spiritual legacy. Though his offer on the property was rejected by the UTS Board of Trustees, our experience with him taught me that God has prepared many to help build a world of love and peace.

God's ideal is that all humanity will connect to create a network of spiritual energy that will unite us and realize God's kingdom on earth. Through this encounter, I understood more than ever that we are not the only ones with this vision. Father and Mother Moon have held a central position in the amazing journey to establish heaven on earth, but God has prepared many to promote this ideal until it becomes reality.

A Revolutionary Movement

In August 2019 at age 74, Hugh retired as president of UTS, his alma mater, but continues to be active in church activities. Hugh had steered the UTS ship through troubled waters, and it was time for someone else to develop the academic curriculum, including a complete online educational program that Hugh had initiated. Hugh is an organizer, manager, and educator. An academician as his successor would take Unification Theological Seminary through the next stage in its development.

Hugh and I had worked for nineteen years as educators at BIA. It was satisfying for us to have spent the better part of two decades investing in the education of youth. Shortly before I retired in June 2016, I was reminded that God had worked beyond the Unification Church by preparing others to join in the effort to build his kingdom. The essence of our Founder's message was that he had not come to start a new religion but to bring all humanity together as one family under God. He himself had worked to bring God's ideal into the realms of religion, education, the media, economics, science, culture and the arts in order to promote world peace.

At the center of everything was the Divine Principle teaching and the ideal of families as the intimate dwelling place of God on earth. The idea that God could dwell on earth in every person, every family, and every facet of society may not be new from a philosophical point of view, but we had been charged to realize this ideal in our lifetimes. In this light, our work in the church, including our work in education, was revolutionary.

CHAPTER 16

Flow of Heart

On a practical level, how can I take part in bringing the kingdom of heaven on earth as I move further into the eighth decade of my life. I have come to believe that my job is to allow God to dwell fully within me and within my interactions with my family, friends, and community. This is easier said than done, but I believe it's an effective way to express my faith and continue kingdom building!

Thoughts and feelings, even good ones, can distract us from the present moment—a place where our energy expands and we sense a close connection to ourselves, to each other, and to God. Even when I consider past events and people, I am drawn to the essence of my experience—the moments when God was most present. Instead of reviewing events, I am noticing connections. When I am with friends and family today, I am more appreciative of the flow of the love and affection that holds us together.

Time to Be

During more than fifty years of marriage, our love for each other has held strong as we weathered the storms of opposition to our church, carried out our missions, experienced challenges of faith, and raised a family. As a safe, solid, faithful man of integrity, Hugh has been an anchor for me. Through all the years, he has been conscientious, sincere, and constant. We have been partners—close and trusted friends. I always appreciated his constant encouragement. He unselfishly supported me in the many missions that I was called to do.

We see our retirement years as a time to enjoy our children and grandchildren. In November 2019, we visited our son High, his wife Kym, and our two grandsons, Brayden and Jaxon, in Florida to explore the possibility of living near them. We bought a house in a 55-plus residential community in Clermont, and one month later, we moved to the sunshine state.

The Joy of Family

Among my earliest friends were my eight siblings. We still today share bonds of friendship, and we love getting together whenever we can. We are there for each other in tangible ways. When we moved to Florida, two of my siblings and their spouses lived nearby in Sarasota, and the siblings in Pennsylvania visited us several times. My brother Reuben (number 5 in the family) recently passed on after battling Alzheimer's disease for the last few years. It was a time when his siblings visited Florida in support of his family, including three of his children and spouses who moved to Sarasota. I should mention here that my brother, Lloyd (number 2), also passed away in 2006. We are now a family of seven living children with our spouses and their children. Still a big family!

We are also very close to Hugh's family and have joyful reunions every three years with his extended family. The Spurgin reunions began with Hugh's parents hosting everyone at the ranch in Missouri. Afterwards, the children and grandchildren continued the tradition. High and Kim hosted the most recent reunion held in Clermont in July 2021. Our other children hosted reunions with the cousins.

We are blessed with four wonderful and talented children: Andrea, Chris, Ameri and High. As fine adults, they are also our friends. The happiness we knew while raising them was mixed with the sadness of separations due to our mission work. During those years, we invited others to share our family's love and care, and our home became a waystation for kids who needed a secure place to stay because of their parents' mission work. We always believed that God was in our lives as well as in theirs, holding us all safely in His embrace.

After more than fifty years of marriage and mission work, we are finding time to relax, to just be in each other's presence, and to share experiences with our family. We enjoy seeing our four children continue to blossom as successful contributors to society, supportive siblings to each other, affectionate children to us, faithful partners in marriages of their own, and loving parents to their own children. We have been blessed to have three grandsons. The eldest, Ari, lives with his parents, Chris and Mary, in Seattle, Washington, while our two younger grandsons, Brayden and Jaxson, live with High and Kym in Florida.

Our family (left to right) front row: Hugh, Ari, Nora, Tim, Andrea (holding Brayden) back row: Chris, Mary, Ameri, High (holding Jaxon) and Kym

Our adult children enjoy one another.

Ari

I realized a number of years ago that it was essential to make the time and effort to spend time with Ari, since we live on opposite coasts. When his mother, a teacher, had to work an extra week after school closed every year, I chose that week to fly to Seattle and care for Ari while his mother completed her reports. It was only one week out of fifty-two, but that time together created a bond between us and gave me a chance to visit with Chris and Mary. During these years, Ari was seven, eight, and nine years old.

Ari's bright eyes would light up as we played together. Every day we packed a sandwich, went for a walk, and found a place to sit and eat our lunch. As we walked and talked, I was so impressed with his curiosity. He noticed everything along the way. Once he said a particular house would look better if it was painted. Then it became a game to look at each house and point out improvements that could be made. It was fascinating to see this little boy's keen sense of beauty. He is a talented artist!

During one visit, we drove together to Idaho to attend Hugh's nephew's wedding. Chris was driving back to Seattle when he was pulled over for exceeding the speed limit. As the officer took his papers back to the patrol car, Chris was upset and remarked that his insurance payments would be increased. I said, "We will send angels to the officer, and maybe he will be inspired to be generous." Chris was not impressed. Ari, however, was listening intently to our exchange.

When the patrol officer returned with the paperwork, he said to Chris, "I am only going to give you a warning this time, but keep in mind that the speed limit is sixty miles per hour on this stretch of the road." Ari had taken in the entire conversation, and we exchanged a smile.

Later, when they dropped me off at the airport, I stood on the sidewalk to wave goodbye. Ari looked out of window of the car and said to me, "May the angels go with you, Grandma!"

Brayden and Jaxon

Living in Clermont gives us opportunities to spend time with Brayden and Jaxon, who live a few minutes away. I have become the "Craft Grandma" by helping them with craft projects. Each is creative in a unique way. Brayden, the future scientist and architect, told me recently, "I have this notebook my mommy gave me for a journal, but I call it my idea book. I want to be an inventor, so every time I get an idea, I draw it in this book."

We have valued every opportunity to spend time with our grandchildren. As we look back at the years in which we sacrificed our time with our children, we feel that one way to serve them now is to care for their children.

A Long Term Connection with Friends

I was blessed to share a deep faith with friends before and after I joined the Unification Church. One circle of friends I have cherished throughout my life is connected by a special letter that has circulated for fifty-eight years. As I have already mentioned, when I was twenty-two years old, I joined Mennonite Voluntary Service and was assigned to work with migrant workers. I left my family and friends in Pennsylvania to live in Homestead, Florida, for a two-year service program. At a goodbye party, my friends decided to start a circle letter to keep us all connected. We made a list of our names and addresses, put it in an envelope, and began sending the envelope around to each person who, in turn, inserted a letter. When the envelope came around again, we replaced our old letter with a new one.

Every six months, we each receive a packet of fourteen letters, and the letters are still making the circuit. Through this small contact, we know about each other's marriages, children, joys, sorrows, and the deaths that have occurred. I think we will continue sending letters until we ourselves die. How precious are friendships!

Church Friends

I met many of the closest friends and colleagues of my adult life in my church, and our shared awareness of God has cemented our friendships. I have worked side by side with intelligent, dedicated, talented, and self-less people and learned much from these connections. Some taught me the Divine Principle, some were role models, some were in my life for a brief time, and others over many years. There are too many to name, but they are all important.

In 1967, when I moved into the church center in Washington another new member, Anne, was living there as well. Later the same year, Betsy joined in New York and came to visit in Washington. Near that time, Marie and her cousin Linna, both teachers, joined the center in Washington. They were members of the Church of the Brethren, which is a denomination that is similar in its beliefs and customs to the Mennonite Church. In different ways, these women were among those who influenced my feeling that I was in the right place.

Through the years, our lives remained intertwined, and we followed many of the same paths in our life of faith. Marie and Linna, along with others in the early church, were married in the 1969 marriage blessing of thirteen couples in America. Betsy, Anne, and I were in the group of seven American couples who participated in the 1970 marriage Blessing Ceremony in Seoul.

Though I haven't kept in close touch with everyone from those early days, they will always be part of my life. Tacco and David, from the 777 couples' group, worked in a distant center, so I rarely saw them, but they later became part of our family when their daughter Mary married our son, Chris!

Most of my close friends in the church shared experiences of leadership. Betsy, Anne, Marie, and I were itinerary workers who traveled around America visiting members in young church centers. All of us, including our husbands, served as church leaders in centers, as itinerary workers, on bus teams, at headquarters, and/or in educational settings. Several of us worked at Camp Sunrise, in the Blessed Family Department, or with WFWP. As we raised our children, we shared the joys and challenges of family life.

Working together in the church brought us close. When our children were young, some of us spent time together as families. When the kids left the nest, and we were more settled, we got together for family vacations and ladies' reunions.

On one occasion, Betsy, Anne, and I rented a bed and breakfast accommodation for a weekend reunion in a lovely Victorian house on the Jersey

Shore and walked along the boardwalk singing old-time songs at the top of our lungs! One night, we were laughing so hard and long that another guest later said she had wanted to knock on our door and join us!

Another time, Betsy, Marie, Anne, and I spent four days in my childhood friend's bed and breakfast on a farm in Pennsylvania. There we shared some of our early childhood experiences and sang together at night while Marie played the guitar.

The Hose, Spurgin, and Jones families spent three days together on the beach in a house Betsy rented on Cape Cod. Sometimes we used our time-shares to vacation together. We spent a week in the beautiful Shenandoah Mountains with our combined families and enjoyed long walks and talks.

In June 2004, the same group used our timeshares to stay side-by-side in a resort in the Pocono Mountains in Pennsylvania. More long walks in the woods and near the Delaware River were highlights. The women tried water aerobics while the men played golf on a mountainous course. Hugh got a hole-in-one! For his birthday, Andrea framed the golf ball and tee with a photo of the course in the background. Our growing or grown children sometimes visited us during our get-togethers and tuned in on some of the stories of our lives.

With our husbands, Anne, Betsy, and I, and another good friend from the early days successfully got together almost every year for a long lunch, when family visits brought us close enough for such gatherings. After Anne and George moved to Arizona, the Jones and Spurgins visited them and other good friends from the early days.

An Alaskan Cruise

In celebration of our fortieth wedding anniversary, Betsy, Anne, and I went with our sweethearts, Farley, George, and Hugh, on an eight-day cruise in June 2010. This was a wonderful time of sharing and exploring the unique beauty of Alaska. The cruise offered us an opportunity to celebrate by having meals together and sightseeing offshore as couples or in groups. Sometimes "the girls" took in events and the "boys" did their own thing. One night we went to hear a band play on the ship, and as we walked in, they were playing "The Anniversary Waltz"!

Hugh and I in Alaska

The next morning, we were greeted with breathtaking views of craggy mountains high above both sides of a narrow waterway. We had our fill of seeing seals on ice floes, imposing glaciers, and frozen waterfalls. It was a most relaxing time, and we all appreciated the chance to catch up on our lives and make new memories.

Birthdays

On my seventieth birthday, Hugh and the children arranged a party with more than eighty relatives and friends at Mary's college in New York. Chris wrote a skit and had everyone laughing. He played the role of the archangel Michael and climbed a ladder to offer me three gifts from God: two angels to give me a massage, a tome revealing all the secrets of the universe, including a chapter on angels, and a clone of me, played by my daughter Ameri. Far-away friends who couldn't attend sent loving messages and photos that the children used in a slide show. On my eightieth birthday, I invited Marie and Betsy to an overnight get-together at my daughter Andrea's house in New Paltz, New York.

Relatives and friends at my 70th birthday celebration in 2008

Betsy, me, and Marie celebrate our friendship on my 80th birthday

The joy of sharing old times, our children's and grandchildren's lives, and our love for each other is deep. We will carry it with us forever.

Living in the Sunshine State

The beautiful blue skies, the lush green lawns, the bright flowers, and the warm weather create a beautiful place to retire. Sometimes, we ride a golf cart to the hilltop by a lake and watch the Florida sunset with other couples from our community.

Hugh and I read and pray together. We have found that many of our neighbors also have a spiritual path and freely share their faith with us. There are always opportunities to share my book on angels. This becomes a great topic of conversation and opens doors to a wide range of conversations and friendships.

Hugh and I at our home in Florida

We are enjoying activities that we never had time for during our five decades of mission work. Having grown up as an avid golfer as a teenager, Hugh had little time for golf while doing church missions. The two golf courses in our community beckon him to meet weekly with friends in a league. I have found a home for my creative interests in a quilters' club, a ceramics club, and a writers' club. I also exercise regularly in a community pool. These activities have provided opportunities for us to meet new friends, and we find that old friends and family like to visit us in our beautiful setting. We are further away from family members and some of our dearest friends. However, during our first few months in Florida, Covid-19 kept everyone conscious of the need to avoid travel. So we learned the value of zoom calls with family, friends, and even church worship services.

We thank God every day to be able to live in this community of wonderful new friends with whom we can share our lives. Some residents refer to our community as "God's waiting room," a place near heaven.

Life moves at a slower pace, and I am finding ways to deepen my sense of God's presence in nature, in others, and in myself. I am only one person, but if I can allow God more room in my heart and in my life, this will positively affect my family, my friends, and everyone and everything around me. In my latter years, this has become my mission.

CHAPTER 17

Being

We must not wait to be

In preparing to be

We must not wait to do

In preparing to do

But in being and doing

prepare for higher being and doing

— Author unknown

My life today is more about *being* than about *doing*. For those of us who have always been doers, like Hugh and I, it takes an adjustment in thinking and even acceptance of self to realize that there is value in the stillness of one's soul—in letting God use us in a different way.

Recently, a close friend passed away at the age of ninety-four. At his funeral, one person commented, "You could always feel his presence in church. Somehow, the service felt different when he was not there." Dr. Edwin Ang, Marie's husband, was a pillar of spiritual strength to many who valued his leadership, kindness, faithfulness, and commitment. Many appreciated and understood that comment. Even at ninety-four, Edwin was still very much a doer, but his life also pointed to the value of being.

I think of the Biblical story of Martha and Mary, sisters who hosted a visit from Jesus. Martha, the doer, was busy serving the meal for Jesus' visit, but Mary sat at Jesus' feet letting her heart of love flow. When Martha complained about Mary not helping her, Jesus responded, "Mary has chosen the greater part."

I am discovering the value of being in a place where God's love can flow freely and deeply, and I can allow things to happen that I do not plan. Sometimes, good things just happen when we are fully present. God can use our spiritual energy to affect the atmosphere around us, and we give of ourselves just by being there.

Allowing God to Lead

My life has been a journey of the evolution of the soul toward oneness with God, our heavenly parent. With each step forward, there was always something more to experience. Stepping into new horizons requires not only a spirit of adventure, but also the humility to make a fresh start—to make a foundation on a new level. The more I'm aware of my connection to God, and the more I allow God to lead, the less I need a roadmap.

Many years ago, I read the book, *Your God is too Small.* "Do not put God in a box," the author advised. I have thought of this advice often over the years, as I sought to give God space to guide my steps and grow unconditional love in my heart.

My Treasure Chest

Hopefully, I have shared a small part in kingdom building by working side by side with our Founders, connecting to their mission to usher in a kingdom of love and peace on earth. My heart is full of gratitude for the life of service that they have lived for humanity.

Events and people in my life stand out like ever-brighter bulbs on the string of Christmas lights, which has helped me find my way forward. I not only know but experience that the source of that light is the flow of divine love from God.

These connections have given me a treasure chest filled to overflowing with precious relationships with family, friends, colleagues, mentors and teachers. In that treasure chest, there are both happy and challenging events that brought joys and sorrows, and there are many lessons learned and taught.

With love, I leave this treasure chest as my legacy.

About the Author

Nora Spurgin grew up in a conservative Mennonite farm family where it was not customary to attend high school. Later she passed a GED test, graduated from Eastern Mennonite College and earned a Masters of Social Work from New York University.

An accomplished speaker, Nora is the author of *Circles of Angels, Insights into the Afterlife* and numerous articles on family life. In addition to her own sense of God's ever present love, the Unification Church and its founders played a central, inspirational role in her peacekeeping efforts toward the building of the Kingdom of Heaven on earth.

Nora served as the National Director of the Family Department of her church where she counseled couples, edited journals and organized educational programs. She traveled throughout America and worldwide in her many missions as a mentor to missionaries and youth leaders.

As president of Womens Federation for World Peace, she promoted peace and bonds of friendship among women of diverse backgrounds. In this role, she met and traveled with entertainers and national leaders. In her later years as the principal of Bridgeport International Academy, she drew on her accumulated experiences to educate teenagers from around the world.

Nora and Hugh, her husband of 52 years, have raised four talented children who now have successful marriages and careers. They are the grandparents of three.

In *Spiritual Connections*, Nora recounts an amazing journey in which God opened doors and lead her to an ever deepening and expanding life of faith and opportunities.